LEARN TO COOK WHEAT, GLUTEN AND DAIRY FREE

100 step-by-step recipes

Antoinette Savill

Grub Street | London

Dedicated to my beautiful daughter,
Sophia

Published by
Grub Street Publishing
4 Rainham Close
London
SW11 6SS
www.grubstreet.co.uk

Copyright this edition © Grub Street 2009
Text copyright © Antoinette Savill 2009
Designed by Lizzie B Design
Photography by Michelle Garrett
Food styling by Jayne Cross

British Library Cataloguing in Publication Data
Savill, Antoinette.
   Learn to cook wheat, gluten and dairy-free : 100
   step-by-step recipes.
   1. Wheat-free diet--Recipes. 2. Gluten-free diet--
Recipes.
   3. Milk-free diet--Recipes.
   I. Title
   641.5'6318-dc22

   ISBN 978-1-906502-50-8

Printed and bound in Malta

Grub Street Publishing uses only FSC (Forest Stewardship
Council) paper for its books.

Contents

INTRODUCTION

Once you are told that you have to follow either a wheat-free, gluten-free or dairy-free diet you begin to work out just what you can safely eat. Even with the huge improvements in the range, texture and taste of allergy-free products it is pretty daunting. There simply are not enough fresh or frozen products that taste nice and there are very few ready-made meals available. The products that are around are often overly sweet or salty to make up for lack of flavour elsewhere and they tend to be expensive. This gives you a very good reason to start cooking allergy-free food at home.

Although the need for allergy-free foods has dramatically increased over the last 5 years, a few of the supermarkets still want long-life products so that they guarantee their profits on what they consider a very small up-take. This of course means that all sorts of additives are used and not only does the integrity of the product suffer but in my opinion our bodies do too. Every nutritionist that I speak to says that "You are what you eat", this being so then I personally do not want all these additives, preservatives and colours on a regular basis. It is worth taking the time to make the products for myself.

Some people find that cooking becomes a tyranny when they have to make big family meals and then a small portion of allergy-free foods for one person. I aim to use recipes that are delicious for all the family or which give you a buzz for entertaining friends. You can work out a balanced compromise between cooking nutritional food at home and using convenience allergy-free foods as back-up when you are zapped of energy or have a sudden change of plan.

More and more people are using convenience foods because of the time pressures of everyday life. For some it is the long working hours and commuting, for others it is the non-stop day looking after a family. Some people just don't like cooking because they have never been shown how to and feel nervous trying new recipes. Of course when you are a beginner cooking does take longer and this also puts people off. Learning to judge when and where you can skip ingredients that you forgot to buy without an ensuing disaster or judging when you can take shortcuts is a skill that develops after a certain amount of experience.

I hope that the easy recipes in this book will help build-up your self-confidence and encourage you to cook so often that you will become swift and stress free in the kitchen.

Cooking really can be a joy even if you only have a small repertoire that you are confident with. You will find that you get a lot of pleasure from creating with your own hands a masterpiece of a pudding or cake, a fabulous warm salad laden with the freshest, finest ingredients or an aromatic spicy dish just waiting to be devoured by your family and friends. The feel-good factor will encourage you to become more adventurous and in no time at all you may even find cooking a therapeutic release from the day-to-day stresses of life.

Glossary

Here is a short list of cookery terms that are frequently used and will be useful to understand before starting to read the recipes if you have never cooked before.

- Al dente is an Italian term for cooking food until it is tender but still firm to the bite, usually applied to pasta and green vegetables.
- Baste means to moisten food with melted fat or a highly flavoured sauce during roasting or grilling.
- Blanch means either to put food in cold unsalted water, bring to the boil, briefly simmer and drain or to put directly into boiling water for a few minutes and drain.
- Braise means cooking whole or large pieces of poultry, fish, game, vegetables or meat in wine, stock or other liquids in a closed pot to help tenderize it.
- Coulis is a smooth or rough textured thin purée which can be poured over savoury or sweet dishes.
- Curdle means to cause sauce, eggs, cake mix or milk to separate into solid and liquid from overheating or an imbalance of ingredients.
- Dice is cutting meat, game, poultry or vegetables into small chunks. They are cube-shaped pieces cut fast and neat.
- Parboil means to partially cook a vegetable so that it can then continue to be cooked in another way.
- Poach refers to cooking in liquid just below simmering point. This is used for fish and fruit that break up easily.
- Refresh means to cool hot food quickly either under cold running water or by plunging in iced water.
- Roasting and baking both refer to cooking in the oven. Roasting is done at high temperature without covering food so that it browns and baking can be covered but is cooked at a lower temperature.
- Sauté is a form of frying; the idea is to keep the food constantly jumping around the pan without too much fat. The food browns and cooks evenly over a high temperature but doesn't stick to the pan.
- Searing and griddling both use the minimal amount of fat on a searingly hot surface, heavy pans are used but a griddling pan is ridged and the searing pan is flat.
- Simmering means to cook something in simmering water, this means that a few small bubbles are making their way to the surface and the surface trembles slightly.
- Stir-fry means to cook small pieces of food with very little fat over very high heat usually in a wok.
- Sweating refers to cooking over low heat, with a small amount of fat and a lid placed tightly on top.
- Zest refers to the thin outer layer of citrus fruits – it can be grated or thinly pared with a vegetable peeler but it must be separated from the bitter white pith underneath.

Kitchen Rules

Here are some simple health and safety rules that will make your kitchen a safe and easy place to work. You don't have to be manic about hygiene just sensible. A little bit of dust or dirt is usually harmless but raw proteins left in a warm place to contaminate other foods is unwise.

- Wash your hands before cooking and after dealing with raw meat, eggs, fish, onions, garlic or chillies.
- When you are cooking turn the saucepan handles to the side so that you do not knock them.
- Have a space ready for hot pots and put them on to a heatproof mat or board
- Keep knives sharp – sharp knives are safer than blunt ones.
- Never leave a sharp knife or processor blade in the washing up bowl or sink where it may not be seen or in a drawer where it may be obscured by other implements.

- Don't wash your sharp knives in the dishwasher as the drying heat affects the metal and blunts them.
- Invest in a large chopping board for fish, poultry, game and meat and another one for all your other ingredients and keep them separate when cooking. I also suggest that you have one just for sweet recipes. The last thing you want is a smelly old bit of garlic in your apple pudding.
- Change tea towels and washing up cloths, brushes and scourers regularly to avoid cross contamination.
- Don't put any warm food in the refrigerator or deep-freeze in case other food deteriorates.
- Wrap up any spare food for the freezer properly or it will get freezer burn.
- Invest in a good pair of oven gloves and never use a damp dishcloth to remove hot objects from the oven.
- I suggest using an oven thermometer to ensure that the oven isn't much hotter than you think and equally fridge and freezer thermometer to prevent too high a temperature which could compromise the household's health.
- If you have a small or cluttered kitchen it is often easier to collect your ingredients together first, measure them out and have them ready in little dishes.

Useful Kitchen Equipment

Always buy the best quality kitchen equipment you can as you definitely get what you pay for. Spend time and enjoy choosing the items you need, then you will enjoy using them.

- Casserole dish – flame and heatproof dishes which can go directly onto heat or into the oven work best. Buy a bigger one which allows plenty of room for the cooking meat and vegetables. Make sure the handles are big enough for you not to lose your grip if it is hot and heavy.
- Chopping boards – get the biggest you can afford – the best are wood and then a few smaller plastic ones are useful.
- A large heavy non-stick frying pan with high sides is indispensable as you can cook chicken dishes as well as having a fry-up.
- A small non-stick frying pan only for pancakes.
- Graters – Microplane graters are great for citrus zest and nutmeg.
- Kitchen tongs are ideal for quickly and easily turning over food without burning yourself.
- Knives – buy the best you can. You will need one big Chef's knife, one small knife and a small serrated knife for tomatoes.
- A knife sharpener – use a hand-held one as recommended by retailer.
- Saucepans – look for solid heavy bases which conduct the heat properly – buy fewer better quality ones.
- Sieves – buy a large metal one, a smaller one and a very small one is useful for icing sugar.
- Colander – big metal one to drain vegetables and pasta.
- Food processor, an electric hand whisk and if you have enough room a liquidiser is far better for making soups and coulis.
- A selection of wooden spoons – change your wooden spoons every year, they only cost a few pounds for a set and then you can keep half of them for sweet recipes only and use the others for all other recipes.
- A pastry brush and a plastic/rubber spatula, a palette knife and a large wooden rolling pin with a set of pastry cutters.
- A selection of non-stick cake tins in 20cm/8in and 23cm/9in sizes and a standard non-stick bread loaf tin. Also choose one muffin tray of 12 holes or 2 x 6 muffin trays for baking tarts and mince pies etc. If you like entertaining then 2 x 12 mini tartlet trays will allow you to make mini quiches, muffins or tartlets.
- If you are starting from scratch you will need

a set of mixing bowls, a lemon squeezer, garlic crusher, a 1 litre/1¾ pint measuring jug and a small and medium balloon whisk.

- To minimize the washing up I suggest using oven to table dishes. Essential for dishes such as lasagne, shepherds pie, apple crumble etc. but also easy for many other dishes. Choose dishes of varying sizes to suit your everyday needs and your usual number of guests when entertaining. There is no point in huge dishes if you are only ever four at a meal. Equally it is a bore to have to use two dishes because they are too small.

The list is endless but this should give you a good start.

The Store Cupboard and Shopping

It is far easier to start allergy-free cooking if you are very organized with a full store cupboard of suitable and useful ingredients. As shopping for allergy-free ingredients can be time consuming it is best to choose a selection of recipes that you will try out in the near future. I always buy some spare packets of tempting nibbles such as allergy-free biscuits, cookies, amaretti biscuits, mini oat cakes and pitta bread and there are products like bread, rolls and muffins which are best frozen. It can be tempting to resort to unsuitable ingredients rather than trek off to the shops so it is advisable to have spare packets of allergy-free flours, pasta and other essentials.

Here is a short list of the most useful products for these recipes.

- Doves Farm gluten-free plain white, self raising flour and white bread flour
- Orgran gluten-free self raising flour
- Pure cornflour
- Glebe Farm bread mixes
- Orgran gluten-free rice crumbs (breadcrumbs substitute)
- Salute gluten-free spaghetti, penne and spirals
- Orgran gluten-free macaroni
- Pure vanilla extract

- Free From pitta breads
- Baking powder and bicarbonate of soda (check labels for allergy-free)
- Lovemore gluten-free frozen puff pastry
- Mustard powder
- Balsamic and wine vinegar
- Ground almonds and ground rice
- Gluten-free lemon cookies and digestive biscuits
- Meridian Free From Tamari soya sauce
- Extra virgin olive and sunflower oil
- Dairy-free sunflower spread and Trex or Cookeen
- Redwoods dairy-free Feta, mozzarella, cheddar and nachos-style cheeses
- Tofutti creamy-style dips, sour cream supreme and ice cream
- Life Free From Parmazano grated hard cheese replacer
- Life Free From Worcester sauce
- Dried chilli flakes, fresh garlic, vanilla pods and whole nutmegs
- Unrefined caster sugar and icing sugar
- Rice: Risotto, short grain white, Easy cook long grain white
- Alpro (Provamel) soya milk and single cream (chiller cabinet)
- Kinnerton Luxury Dark Chocolate

Oven Temperatures

Mark 3 | 325F | 170C

Mark 4 | 350F | 180C

Mark 5 | 375F | 190C

Mark 6 | 400F | 200C

Mark 7 | 425F | 220C

Please note that throughout all the recipes I use a 20ml tablespoon measure so if you use a 15ml measure then be generous with the amounts.

All eggs used in the recipes are free-range and organic and all olive oil used is extra virgin but I have left it to you to make your own choices.

SOUPS

Soup is so versatile it can be a hearty warming lunch dish with a hunk of bread and cheese or a colourful and subtle starter to a dinner party. You can make a cheap soup from all the weekend's leftover vegetables or a more expensive fish soup to replace a main course.

Soup you can make at home is really divided into two categories, a liquidised soup of cooked vegetables processed into a smooth purée or a chunky, meal-in-a-bowl type soup with fish, game or poultry.

To make a good soup you need to extract the deepest flavour you can from the vegetables and you need to be able to judge whether to thicken or thin down the soup without losing the depth of flavour or the texture. Your background flavour is what starts off the soup so this is important. It is the part that you don't want to skip. This is usually onion, oil and garlic, spices or herbs. The main ingredients are then the predominant flavour and the aromatics should be merely complimentary not overpowering. All soups need some liquid of course and seasoning and a good home-made stock is an easy and healthy option.

The art of a good soup is undoubtedly the sweating of the vegetables first. This means that you cook the onions and oil (and herbs, spices or garlic) in a pan with the lid on over very low heat for about 15 minutes. You will need to stir the onions once or twice but they should produce enough liquid to prevent them from sticking or burning.

The soup needs to be thickened somehow, to give it body and structure. This usually means using a starchy vegetable such as potato or parsnip but can also be rice or pulses.

It is very important that the type of liquid used is in harmony with the other ingredients. You are in fact, diluting the ingredients so although you can use water where the depth of flavour is very intense or dairy-free milk in some cases, the best liquid to use is stock. The stock should not dominate the soup but equally it is the backbone of the soup and should support the flavours. Stock cubes or powders rarely do this although the ready-made chilled stock is fine although you don't actually know anything about the chickens that have been used to make it. So unless the stock happens to be organic, I personally would rather make my own.

Here is the classic and simple recipe for making stock. The more bones and bits of meat that are in the stock the stronger the flavour will be and so the less cooking time it will need.

I like smooth soups the most so a liquidiser is vital to me but a purée can easily be made in a food processor with the metal blade. If you are short of kitchen space then a hand-held wand liquidiser is the best solution. On a safety note: Always make sure that the soup is cool enough not to burn you if you get splashed by the wand and equally ensure that the jug liquidiser is only 3/4 full and that the lid is tightly clamped on before starting the power.

STOCK

To avoid the lingering smell of stock I bring it to the boil on top of the oven and cook it in the oven for the remaining time. You can use any fowl or game birds. For the vegetable stock, use a selection of green vegetables such as courgettes, beans, peas in the pod etc., but keep away from cabbage, broccoli and sprouts which will give an unpleasant bitter flavour. Avoid starchy vegetables which will make a cloudy glutinous gloop of a soup! The better the selection of vegetables the more balanced the taste of the stock will be. Brassicas pong when overcooked which is why you want to avoid them.

CHICKEN STOCK

Makes at least 1 litre/13/4 pints

1 leftover organic free-range chicken
    carcass, raw or cooked
1 onion, peeled and quartered and studded
    with 4 whole cloves
1 large carrot, peeled and quartered
1 leek, topped and tailed, sliced thickly,
    washed under cold running water and
    left to dry in a colander until needed

1 celery stalk, trimmed and thickly sliced
2 bay leaves
1 sprig of thyme
8 black peppercorns and pinch of sea salt

1) Put all the ingredients together in a large pan and add enough boiling water to cover them completely. Add any gravy or pan juices leftover from the roasted birds but scrape off any excess fat first.
2) Bring to the boil over high heat and then either turn down the heat to low and simmer gently for 4 hours or transfer to an oven at 200C/400F/Gas 6 and cook for the same length of time.
3) Check the water every hour and add more hot water to keep the level the same. The oven method avoids smells and any boiling over.
4) Cool and then strain the ingredients. Chuck out the ingredients and cool the stock until cold enough to refrigerate. The stock will keep for 2 days in the refrigerator.

VEGETABLE STOCK

Makes at least 1 litre/1 3/4 pints

1 large onion, peeled and roughly chopped
1 large carrot, peeled and roughly chopped
1 large leek, cleaned, trimmed and roughly
   chopped
2 celery stalks, sliced
2 bay leaves

1 large thyme sprig
3 parsley sprigs
10 black peppercorns
Optional: **pinch sea salt and 1 large clove**
   garlic, peeled

1) Follow the recipe for chicken stock but only cook for 3 hours.

Alternatively, bring the stock to the boil in a large pan and cook until the volume is reduced
by two thirds and then leave to cool. Pour the stock into ice cube containers and freeze them.
Pop the frozen cubes out and into freezer bags, seal and label until needed for sauces,
soups and gravies.

FINISHING TOUCHES

Here are a few ideas once you have made and served the soup.
To dress it up a bit for a special occasion you can try these options.

- •• A swirl of dairy-free soya single cream.
- •• A pinch of freshly chopped parsley, chives or coriander on top of the cream or
  instead of the cream. They should be finely chopped and shouldn't dominate
  the flavour of the soup.
- •• Dairy-free Parmazano grated cheese replacer, goats' or pecorino cheese is great
  on top of chunky vegetable and/or pasta soups.
- •• Flavoured oils can be dribbled into these sorts of soup too.
- •• Lastly, and very popular are croûtons. There is a quick and easy way to make
  them on page 113

SMOOTH CARROT AND RICE SOUP

This soup is very subtle and sophisticated and so it needs the firm backbone of a home-made stock which will give it depth and strength. Serves 4-6

1 large onion, finely chopped
750g/1lb10oz peeled carrots, finely chopped
2 tablespoons olive oil
1.25 litres/2 pints/5 cups home or shop-made chicken stock or gluten-free brand

3 heaped tablespoons short grain white rice
2 tablespoons of freshly chopped coriander leaves
Sea salt and freshly ground black pepper
2 tablespoons of freshly chopped parsley

1) Gently cook the onion and carrots together in the oil until softened but not browned.
2) Add the stock and rice. Bring to the boil; reduce heat to medium and simmer the soup for about 30 minutes or until the rice and vegetables are cooked through.
3) When the soup is cool, process it in a blender with the coriander until smooth.
4) Reheat the soup, season according taste and serve hot, sprinkled with the chopped parsley.

SWEET POTATO AND COCONUT SOUP

Funnily enough the sweet potato is not a potato at all and there are usually two types that we get here in the UK. It is important to check which type you are buying, the white fleshed potato is sticky and starchy and stays firm when cooked. The orange fleshed potato is soft and sweet when cooked. Always buy them with smooth skins and never with damp spots or wrinkles. To avoid colour and texture changes always cook them as a vegetable with their skins on and peel afterwards. Serves 8

1 very large onion, roughly chopped
About 1kg/2lb 2oz/4 large organic sweet potatoes, peeled and cut into chunks
2 tablespoons olive oil
2 heaped teaspoons ground cumin
2 heaped teaspoons ground coriander
1 heaped tablespoon freshly grated organic root ginger
A pinch of dried chilli flakes or 1/2 finely chopped red chilli (medium hot

and deseeded)
4 teaspoons allergy-free vegetable stock powder with 1.5 litres/6 cups boiling water or use a fresh stock
30g/1oz fresh coriander, chopped (reserve 1/2 for decoration)
400ml/14oz can coconut milk
Finely grated rind and juice of 1 unwaxed lime

1) Gently cook the onion and potato in the oil over medium heat for about five minutes.
2) Add the cumin, coriander, ginger and chilli and continue to cook for a minute or two.
3) Sprinkle the potatoes with the stock powder, pour over the water and bring to the boil. Reduce the heat a little and allow the soup to simmer for about 45 minutes until the potatoes are very soft.
4) Add half the coriander leaves and leave the soup to cool.
5) Transfer to a blender or food processor, add the coconut milk and blend until smooth.
6) Transfer the soup back to the saucepan, add the grated lime and juice and reheat.

GREEN MINESTRA

This is a lovely summer soup especially when made with local fresh produce from the farmers' market or your own hand picked garden vegetables. I use red-skinned potatoes because they are particularly starchy and thicken the soup. It is the pesto that gives the soup its texture and flavour, so don't try to leave it out or it will be very unexciting! Serves 4

Vegetable Stock 1 litre/1³/4 pints/4 cups,
   recipe page 10
Rocket Pesto recipe page 46
For the soup
1 bunch spring onions, trimmed
1 trimmed celery heart
1 courgette, topped and tailed

1 large red skinned potato, peeled
80g/3oz French beans, topped and tailed
2 handfuls fresh spinach leaves, washed
2 tablespoons olive oil
100g/3¹/2oz freshly prepared peas
100g/3¹/2oz baby broad (fava) beans
80g/3oz runner beans cut into diamonds

1) Make the vegetable stock recipe and while it is cooking make the rocket pesto recipe and set it aside.
2) Chop the spring onions and celery roughly along with the courgette, potato, French beans and spinach leaves. All the chopped vegetables should be roughly the same size.
3) Put the oil into a thick–based pan over medium heat and gently sweat the onions and celery for a few minutes. Add the potatoes and cook for a few more minutes and then toss in all the remaining vegetables.
4) Pour over the stock and bring the soup to the boil over higher heat and cook until the potatoes are just soft.
5) Serve immediately in hot soup bowls with a large dollop of pesto on each one.

EGGS

There is an amazing display of eggs for sale in the shops. Rare breed hens produce enchanting blue eggs. Organic free-range eggs are easily available now and lots of farms or small holdings sell delicious freshly laid eggs. If you have your own hens, then of course the taste and colour is magic.

Eggs are sorted into sizes, which makes it much easier when shopping. Usually recipes are based on medium-sized eggs stipulating large when called for. So it is worth checking in your cookbook if you are about to make a cake or soufflé when the texture and rising factor is all important.

If you are at all doubtful about the freshness of an egg there is a simple way to check. If the egg is fresh when you crack it into a saucer the yolk should stand proud above the white which clings thickly around it. An older egg will be flatter and flabbier with a more liquid white.

All eggs that are stamped with the lion symbol come from flocks which have been vaccinated against salmonella and are regularly checked. Local eggs should be carefully washed in cold water so that it is safer to crack and use the raw egg. Fresher eggs are easier to crack than older ones.

Store your eggs in a cool larder or the refrigerator and leave them at room temperature for $^1/_4$ - $^1/_2$ hour before using.

When you need to separate eggs in a recipe for the first time it may be best to practice with a few spare ones first. Usually the recipe will suggest one large bowl for the egg whites and one smaller one for the egg yolks. Until you are a dab hand at separating eggs it is a really good idea to have another small dish or bowl for any mistakes. The vital thing is not to let any egg yolk into the whites or the whites will not whisk up properly. Egg yolks are very fatty and this is the reason why the whites won't whisk properly if contaminated. Also, ensure that the bowl is clean with no trace of fat.

To separate the egg: hold it comfortably and tap the exposed side firmly against the side of the bowl. A narrow-edged bowl is better than one with a thick rim. If you are too forceful the whole egg will smash and bits of shell and yolk will contaminate your whites. Carefully ease the shell apart with the tips of your thumbs and pull the two halves apart over the bowl. Some of the whites will fall in but keep the egg yolk in one half of the shell. Gently tip the yolk into the other half and let the white drop into the bowl. Repeat this a few times and then slide the egg yolk gently into its bowl.

Egg whites are whisked to trap small bubbles of air within to make foam. The more the eggs are whisked the thicker and more solid the foam becomes. This foam is used to lighten cakes, mousses and soufflés. Watch out for over-whisking because the eggs can turn lumpy and it becomes very difficult to incorporate them into the recipe.

I always use an electric whisk but a balloon whisk is successful. To whisk more easily tilt your bowl slightly with one hand and whisk with the other. Use your wrist to make circular movements and keep going!

There are 2 stages usually mentioned in recipes:

- • 'Soft peak' which means the whites form a peak but flop over when the whisk is withdrawn
- • 'Firm peak' which means the whites form a peak and remain pointing upwards when the whisk is removed.

If the egg whites just slump back into the bowl and don't peak at all they are not ready – keep going, otherwise they will collapse and liquefy. You cannot re-whisk the egg whites.

To fold egg whites into the recipe always use a metal spoon, this keeps the damage to the foam to the minimum. You are trying to keep as much air as you can to keep the mixture light. You need to use a scooping action and not a stirring action. Take just a spoonful of whites and stir it into your base mixture. The mixture should be tepid. This will loosen it up and make it easier to fold in the remaining egg whites. It also helps if you turn the bowl as you are folding in. Work fast but carefully.

There are recipes with eggs in all through the book but here are few to start off with so that you can easily look through the hints and information.

EGG WHITES

The most well known recipe using egg whites is a meringue mixture. Once you can make the basic meringue you can add brown sugar or nuts, cocoa powder, vanilla, coffee, even lime zest and brown sugar! The opportunities for puddings are endless and of course there is the famous pavlova filled with cream and soft fruits. For those of us on dairy-free diets I suggest using vanilla soya ice cream as the filling for a pavlova. Simply have your fruits ready in bowls, your pavlova on a serving dish and then at the last minute assemble the pudding by scooping one or two tubs of dairy-free ice cream into the middle of the meringue and then heaping the prepared fruit onto it. Individual meringues are harder to fill but again I use dairy-free ice cream and serve them with a lovely raspberry, butterscotch or chocolate sauce. You can find two of these recipes in the sauce section on page 47. Serve both immediately.

The rules for making meringue can be bent or even broken but for the safest bet always make them with 55g/2oz/$^{1}/_{4}$ cup caster sugar to each egg white. There are three types of meringue, Swiss which is the type we use here, Italian which is made with sugar syrup for a crisper and more powdery meringue and meringue cuite which is egg whites and icing sugar whisked over gentle heat and has a fine chalky texture.

Some people prefer white meringues but I love the off-white ones with crisp outside and melting inside. The art is to prevent them weeping and being too chewy.

MERINGUE

PAVLOVA

This delicious pudding from Australia uses cornflour and vinegar but you can make a simpler version just using this basic meringue mixture. If you want to make the original from another recipe remember to use wine vinegar and not malt and pure cornflour. If you are using whipped cream you will need 275ml/^{1}/$_2$ pint for a small pavlova and double the amount for a large one. I suggest preparing about 350g/12oz of mixed raspberries, strawberries and redcurrants for the filling unless you are doubling the recipe.

Decorate with a sprinkling of sifted icing sugar and serve.

A good tip is to make the pavlova the evening before and leave it in the turned-off oven overnight which will dry it out perfectly. Store in a sealed container or wrapped in cling film until needed.

All ages seem to love meringues, they should be light and melting on the outside but slightly chewy on the inside otherwise they can taste too dry.

Make the basic mixture and, using two spoons to shape them, spoon dessertspoonfuls onto a baking sheet. The cooking time is the same. When they are cool, sandwich them together with the ice cream.

BASIC MERINGUE MIX

To make a small pavlova for 6 or 12-16 meringues for 6-8 people use the following amounts. For a large pavlova to serve 10-12 and about 24 meringues double the ingredients.

3 large fresh egg whites
175g/6oz/scant cup caster sugar

•• Preheat the oven to 150C/300F/Gas 2.

1) Cover a lightly oiled baking sheet or non-stick sheet with silicone paper, which peels off very easily. Draw a 20cm/8in circle for the small size pavlova and draw around a 25cm/10in dinner plate for the large pavlova.
2) Use a large clean and dry bowl and have the sugar already measured out.
3) Whisk the eggs until they form soft peaks and you can turn the bowl upside down without them sliding out! Make sure you don't over-beat them or they will do the opposite and collapse.
4) Whisk in 30g/1oz of sugar or simply a tablespoon at a time, whisk after each addition until all the sugar is used up.

For the pavlova:

1) Use a metal spoon to spoon the mixture onto the prepared sheet.
2) Spoon blobs of meringue next to each other all around the edge of the circle so that they join up to make a thick and swirly wall and fill in with a shallow base that you can lightly smooth over.
3) Decorate the wall of the pavlova by lightly swirling upwards with the tip of a knife to make little peaks.

For the meringues:

1) Spoon 12 heaped tablespoonfuls or 16 dessertspoons of the meringue mixture, using two spoons to shape them onto a non-stick baking sheet. No need to use the paper unless your baking sheet is not stable.

Both:

1) Place in the oven and reduce the heat to 140C/275F/Gas 1 and leave to cook for 1 hour if it is the smaller pavlova and the meringues in one or two batches. Allow 1¹/2 hours for the big pavlova.
2) Turn off the heat and leave the pavlova or meringues until completely cold.
3) Peel the paper off the pavlova and store in an air-tight container for up to 2 weeks or freeze for up to a month. This is the same for the meringues.

EGG WHITES AND YOLKS

Omelettes are of course a fantastic fast food, they are easy to make and you don't need a special omelette pan. A good thick-based non-stick frying pan is all that is needed but the critical thing is the size. You should use a 17-20cm/7-8in pan for a 3 egg omelette and a 25cm/10in pan for 6 egg omelette. If the pan is too big it will produce a thin, tough omelette and if the pan is too small it is most likely that the base of the omelette will burn and stick before the middle is cooked enough.

There are four main steps to a perfect omelette:

- • Use butter or dairy-free spread and not oil for a classic French omelette.
- • Do not add water or milk to the eggs to make them go further.
- • Don't over-cook the omelette; the top should be a little bit runny.
  The omelette will carry on cooking whilst you are serving it and it will become rubbery if overcooked.
- • Never keep the omelette waiting, have the filling and any accompanying salad ready and eat immediately.

MUSHROOM AND FETA FRITTATA

A frittata is an Italian omelette which is in between a classic French omelette and a chunky Spanish tortilla. The filling is in the middle and the eggs are usually flavoured with Parmesan or herbs. The frittata is cooked top and bottom and served cut into wedges, like a cake. This makes it ideal for a picnic or lunch box as well as a starter. Frittata is usually cooked in butter but here you can use oil as it is less likely to burn, and it is healthier.

Choose your own mixtures of fillings to suit the season and mood. Serves 4

4 medium sized potatoes, peeled and quartered (450g/1lb)

8 large eggs

1 heaped tablespoon dairy-free Parmazano cheese (see stockists) or either goats' or pecorino cheese

Sea salt and freshly ground black pepper

A pinch of freshly grated nutmeg

1 tablespoon olive oil plus extra for serving

4 spring onions, trimmed and finely sliced

1 large garlic clove, peeled and finely chopped

115g/4oz button mushrooms, wiped clean, trimmed and sliced

2 or 3 heaped tablespoons chopped The Redwood Co. Greek-style dairy-free cheese (drained of oil if in a tub) or either goats' or ewes' cheese

To serve: 4 handfuls of mixed rocket and spinach leaves

1) Cook the potatoes in boiling water until tender. Drain them in a colander, leave to cool and then cut them into bite size pieces.
2) Beat the eggs in a bowl using a fork and mix in the Parmazano, salt, pepper and nutmeg.
3) Heat a 25cm/10in frying pan over medium heat. Add the oil and heat through.
4) Quickly stir in the spring onions, garlic and mushrooms.
5) Once the mushrooms have softened, gently distribute all the ingredients evenly around the pan and sprinkle with the potatoes.
6) Quickly give the eggs a last whisk and then pour them into the pan, tilting and swirling the pan so that the egg settles evenly. Scatter over the cubes of cheese.
7) Leave the frittata to cook for about 5 minutes. Preheat the grill. The top of the frittata should still be runny but the base and sides cooked. Slide the pan under the grill and cook until the top is set and golden brown.
8) Carefully slide the frittata from the pan onto a large plate and serve immediately or leave to cool but serve at room temperature.
9) Arrange the spinach and rocket leaves on four plates and place a wedge of frittata on each one. Drizzle the leaves with a little olive oil and serve.

MAYONNAISE

Mayonnaise is a handy dressing to be able to make and it is the base of some well known dishes. Aioli sauce for example is one of the best known and is served with raw vegetables called crudités or with seafood. Sauce tartare is usually served with fish or fishcakes. It is difficult to make for coeliacs because the main ingredients of gherkins and capers are pickled in vinegar and so a thorough check has to be made that the pickling ingredient is wine vinegar and not malt vinegar.

Curdling occurs if you add the oil too fast at the beginning. If that does happen, it can sometimes be rescued. Take a clean bowl, add a fresh egg yolk, whisk in the curdled mixture drop by drop and then carry on as before. Mayonnaise can be kept for a week in a sealed jar in the refrigerator.

It is a good idea to keep a jar of mayonnaise handy for snacks and meals such as salads, prawn cocktail recipes, sandwiches and stuffed baked potatoes.

I am always amazed at the price of a really good mayonnaise.
It is far cheaper to make it, especially in summer when we probably use much more. Then you can have fun adding lovely flavours like chilli and garlic.

You can serve the mayonnaise in various ways, here are some easy ideas:

- · Mix some mayonnaise with some gluten-free Worcester sauce, tomato ketchup, a pinch of cayenne pepper and lemon or lime juice to taste to make a lovely coating sauce for prawns on a salad.
- · Mix some mayonnaise with finely chopped fresh parsley and chives in a bowl and then pour in a little very hot water beating all the time with a hand whisk until you have a thick and smooth sauce. This is a real cheat but is great with fish cakes or poached fish and chicken.

BASIC MAYONNAISE

2 large egg yolks
1 teaspoon mustard powder
Sea salt and freshly ground black pepper
125ml/4fl.oz/1/2 cup sunflower oil and
   125ml/4fl.oz /1/2 cup olive oil

60ml/2fl.oz/1/4 cup of oil to suit your
   taste
3 teaspoons white wine vinegar

1) To make by hand: put the egg yolks in a glass bowl, add the mustard, a very little salt and pepper and mix with a balloon whisk.
2) Put the oils into a jug and then pour a few drops into the egg mixture. Whisk it in and repeat the process about six times.
3) This will ensure the mixture will begin to thicken and you can start adding larger drops of oil.
4) Whisk in thoroughly each time. When about a quarter of the oil is in then add a teaspoon of vinegar to loosen the mayonnaise.

5) Now you can pour a trickle of oil into the eggs, whisking each time. When another quarter of the oil is used up add another teaspoon of vinegar, mix and continue. When the oil is finished, season with more salt and pepper, the last of the vinegar and transfer to a serving bowl.

•• For an Aioli sauce simply pound a couple of cloves of garlic (or more if you like) with a mortar and pestle to a paste with 1/2 teaspoon coarse sea salt and mix with the basic recipe.
•• Store the mayonnaise in a 450g/1lb screw-top jam jar in the refrigerator until needed, but no longer than a week.

QUICK HOLLANDAISE SAUCE

This is my version of cheating hollandaise sauce and it has done me brilliantly for 25 years. It doesn't matter if you make it in a food processor or a liquidiser or in a bowl with a hand-held electric whisk. Serves 4

115g/4oz dairy-free sunflower spread
2 large egg yolks
1 dessertspoon white wine vinegar

1 teaspoon lemon juice
A pinch of sea salt and freshly ground
    black pepper

1) Put the sunflower spread into a small pan and melt over medium heat until boiling.
2) Meanwhile blend the egg yolks with the vinegar, lemon juice and seasoning in the mini bowl of a food processor.
3) Pour the boiling fat in a steady stream through the funnel into the eggs, blending all the time until the sauce is thick.
4) Transfer the hollandaise sauce to a warm serving bowl and serve tepid.

MINT HOLLANDAISE SAUCE

•• Add 2 heaped tablespoons of chopped fresh mint leaves to the finished sauce. Give it a final blend in the processor.

Note: If the sauce is not thick enough simply transfer the hollandaise into a small pan and cook for a few minutes over very low heat, stirring all the time. The sauce must not get hot or it will separate. Once it is thick transfer immediately into a cold serving bowl or jug and then serve. In an emergency you can return the separated hollandaise to the food processor bowl and blend with another fresh egg yolk to bring it back together again.

CUSTARD

The finest pouring custard is made from egg yolks, milk/cream and sugar and a little vanilla. If the custard is over-heated it will curdle and this is time consuming to restore and a huge cause for anxiety and trepidation. Here I have added a little cornflour to stabilize the sauce, it is not as perfect but worth the peace of mind. Remember that custard should not be too thick to pour. If you need solid custard for a trifle then add a spoon of cornflour and an extra egg yolk to the recipe.

Check that the custard is the correct consistency by looking at the back of the wooden spoon. It should be thinly coated, run your finger down it, and it will leave a clear trail through the custard if it is thick enough. Makes 850ml/1^1/$_2$ pints

600ml/22fl.oz/2^1/$_2$ cups unsweetened dairy-free soya milk
1 vanilla pod cut and opened out lengthways or 2 teaspoons pure vanilla extract
3 large egg yolks

70g/3oz/^{1}/$_3$ cup unrefined golden caster sugar
1 tablespoon pure cornflour

1) Pour the milk into a thick-based pan, add the vanilla pod and simmer gently over low heat until the milk reaches boiling point.
2) Meanwhile, put the egg yolks, sugar and cornflour into a food processor and blend until pale and smooth.
3) Remove the pan from the heat and leave to cool for 5 minutes before removing the vanilla pod.
4) With the food processor running, pour in the milk blending all the time. Add the vanilla extract if you haven't used a pod and blend on pulse repeatedly over the next few minutes.
5) Transfer the custard back to the pan, cook over low heat, stirring all the time, until thick and smooth. If it is frothy keep checking the consistency underneath.
6) Remove the custard from the heat as it reaches boiling point. It must come to boiling point so that the cornflour cooks.
7) Quickly pour the custard into a big jug or bowl to prevent it cooking further.
8) Transfer the custard to a warm jug and serve.

•• A good tip for keeping the custard for later is to cover the surface of the sauce with greased baking parchment, cover with cling film and chill until needed. To reheat, remove the parchment and cling film. Warm through over low heat in a thick-based pan, stirring all the time.

STARTERS

Soups of course make very good starters but when something more solid is needed then you have to plan carefully. It is worth pointing out that you don't want a big heavy starter before a very rich or heavy main course otherwise your guests might not have room for any pudding or cheese. Equally a light starter before a light main course may leave people feeling peckish which will be grumbled about later on the way home! Try and work out a good balance.

Another point to make is that it is not such a good idea to have similar foods at each course and it makes for a much more exciting meal if the flavours and textures contrast nicely and the colours are interesting. For example, avoid having a smoked salmon or fish starter followed by fresh salmon or other fish. A game terrine followed by roast duck or grilled goats' cheese salad followed by a roast vegetable and goats' cheese pasta!

It is worth thinking about the vegetables too. If you are having a salad-based main course or steak and salad you don't want to have grilled goats' cheese or roast vegetables on a salad as a starter. If you choose to have a big hearty casserole or shepherds pie filled with carrots and parsnips, avoid repeating as a soup or part of the starter.

Presentation is as important as the food itself and the starter is leading the guests into a state of expectation for what is to follow, so wow them with the simplest of things. It is far better to have a plate of hors d'oeuvres or fresh crudités and dips that is temptingly arranged than something you have slaved over but plonked on a plate without any care. If time is short then cheat – everyone else does!

Here are a selection of hot or warm starters, these can mainly be prepared in advance and then there is a flurry of last minute activity before the starter is ready to serve. I think you have to be a very experienced and confident cook to produce hot soufflés from scratch so I have not suggested this.

The remaining recipes are cold starters. This does not necessarily mean that they need to be chilled, in fact quite often the starter has to be served at room temperature because cold kills the flavour of so many fresh foods.

Cold starters can often be prepared well in advance which is a life-saver if you are working, have another meal to cook for children before your guests arrive or if you are a bit nervous about cooking. Cover the dishes tightly so that they don't get contaminated by lingering smells in the refrigerator overnight. If you are running very late I suggest you concentrate on the food and leave the laying of the table and the wine to the guests!

These starters are a bit more adventurous and need a little bit of planning. If time is short but you have the space I suggest doing the shopping the day before and laying the table, getting the wines ready and flowers if you are doing them. This leaves you free to spend the time needed on the food preparation. Check the recipe when you are shopping for ingredients and see if there is any part of the recipe you can make in advance. For example, peppers or pine nuts can be roasted, cooled and covered. You can also make and lightly bake pastry the day before needed, as long as it is well wrapped in cling film and then you can assemble the starter at the last minute.

WRAPPED ASPARAGUS WITH QUICK HOLLANDAISE SAUCE

Choose firm thick asparagus and check that none of the tips have been damaged or are going dry or mouldy. Keep them in a cool place until ready to cook. Serves 4 as a starter or 2 for main course

455g/1lb fresh asparagus, trimmed
Quick Hollandaise Sauce recipe page 21

4 large fresh slices Serrano ham
Olive oil and freshly ground black pepper

1) Blanch the asparagus in boiling water for about 7 minutes, drain and plunge into a bowl of cold water.
2) Start making the hollandaise sauce as instructed in the recipe.
3) Drain the asparagus, divide the spears into 4 portions and wrap each portion tightly in a slice of ham.
4) Place on a baking tray, brush with oil and grill until the ham is crispy.
5) Serve the bundles of asparagus on warm plates, drizzle the tips with the sauce and dust with a little black pepper. Serve immediately.

EGGS BENEDICT

I can never manage this wonderful dish for breakfast but I do love it for brunch or a lunch with a sharp frisee and chicory salad and a glass of chilled white wine. If the ham is thin then use 2 slices on top of each other. Serves 4 as a starter or 2 as a main course

Quick Hollandaise Sauce recipe page 21
2 or 4 very thick slices gluten-free white
   bread, crusts removed (see stockists)
2 or 4 thick slices of ham (check it is
   allergy-free)

2 or 4 medium eggs
Dairy-free sunflower spread
Freshly ground black pepper

1) Make the Quick Hollandaise Sauce recipe first and keep it tepid.
2) Use a large (10cm/4in) round metal pastry cutter to cut a circle out of each slice of bread. Use the same cutter to cut enough circles of ham. Poach the eggs in egg poachers or in simmering water until the whites are firm but the yolks are soft.
3) Meanwhile, toast the bread lightly on both sides. Place on warm plates and spread with the sunflower spread.
4) Place a piece of ham on each circle of toast. Place the egg on top and pour over some hollandaise sauce. Dust with black pepper and serve immediately.

CHICKEN LIVER PARFAIT WITH CRANBERRY AND WALNUT SALAD

I quite often divide the pâté into oval shaped moulds or even square ones. I then serve them on a similar shaped white plate which looks great for a dinner party. You can make them a day in advance. Makes 8-12

900g/2lb fresh or defrosted chicken livers, sinews or fat removed, rinsed under cold running water in a fine sieve and drained
1 large onion, finely chopped
3 tablespoons olive oil
150g/5oz dairy-free sunflower spread
Sea salt and freshly ground black pepper
Plenty of freshly ground nutmeg
2 heaped teaspoons each of fresh marjoram leaves, thyme leaves and chopped sage leaves or 1 teaspoon of each if using dried herbs

2 cloves garlic, chopped
3 tablespoons medium dry sherry
4 tablespoons dairy-free soya single cream

Walnut and cranberry salad
115g/4oz each of chopped walnuts and dried cranberries
Walnut oil and balsamic vinegar
Sea salt and freshly ground black pepper
4 tablespoons of finely chopped parsley

•• You will need 8 lightly oiled tins or 12 x oval rubber moulds tray or small ramekins with a circle of greaseproof paper placed in the bottom.

1) Put the prepared livers into a large bowl, use clean fingers to separate them and leave to one side.

2) In a large frying pan, gently cook the onions in the oil until softened but not browned. Stir in the livers and 30g/1oz of the sunflower spread and cook until browned all over.

3) Now add the salt, pepper, nutmeg, herbs, chopped garlic and sherry. Shake the pan from time to time until the livers are cooked through but just a tiny bit pink in the middle.

4) Remove the pan from the heat and leave the mixture to cool. Scrape the mixture into a food processor and blend until fairly smooth. Add the remaining sunflower spread, whiz again until smooth. Add the cream and blend briefly.

5) Adjust the seasoning to taste and scrape the mixture into the prepared moulds or ramekins and level off the tops. Cover and chill until needed.

6) Roast the walnuts in a little walnut oil in a medium hot oven until golden. Meanwhile, pour boiling water to cover over the cranberries and leave them for 5 minutes, drain and then combine with the warm nuts.

7) Toss the nuts in 3 tablespoons of walnut oil and a drizzle of balsamic vinegar and season with a little salt and pepper. Mix in the chopped parsley and then cover until needed.

8) Turn the parfaits out into the centre of 8-12 small plates. Spoon the walnut and cranberry salad about half way around each one and serve with allergy-free toast or bread rolls.

ROAST FIGS WITH PROSCIUTTO AND CHEESE

This is a blissfully simple Italian recipe which barely needs cooking and is therefore ideal as a summer starter for eight or even a main course for four. If the figs are tiny then you would need two each. Serves 4 or 8

8 ripe large figs

8 heaped teaspoons Tofutti Creamy Smooth Original cream cheese alternative or either soft goats' or ewes' cheese

8 slices Italian prosciutto (dry cured ham)

4 or 8 handfuls washed wild rocket leaves

A drizzle of balsamic vinegar and olive oil

Freshly ground black pepper

1) Carefully wipe the figs clean with wet kitchen roll. Carefully slice about 3/4 the way down each fig from the stalk to the base and again so that you have quarters that can be gently pushed back.

2) Pile a spoonful of cream cheese into the centre of each fig. Gently close up the fig around the cheese and wrap up carefully but tightly with a slice of ham. It should be secure.

3) Place the figs on a non-stick baking tray and grill under high heat until the cheese is hot and the ham crispy round the edges.

4) Divide the rocket onto 4 or 8 plates and place the hot figs on top. Drizzle the leaves with the vinegar and oil and season with a little black pepper and serve immediately.

SPRING ROLLS WITH CHILLI SAUCE

Home-made spring rolls seem a bit alarming but in fact they are easy to make. They are a great snack or starter and you can also make a peanut sauce for dipping. I suggest keeping a few packets of wraps in your cupboard. If you use the smaller 50g/2oz packet you will need two of them. Makes 12 large rolls

Dipping sauce

2 tablespoons Meridian Free From Tamari
   soya sauce
2 tablespoons tomato ketchup
1/2 medium red chilli, halved, deseeded and
   finely chopped

Rolls

100g/3^{1}/2oz beansprouts
55g/2oz cabbage, shredded
1 large carrot, peeled and cut into
   matchsticks
1/2 red pepper, deseeded and thinly sliced
6 spring onions, trimmed, very thinly sliced
1 clove garlic, crushed
2.5cm/1in piece root ginger, peeled and
   grated
1 tablespoon Meridian Free From Tamari
   soya sauce
12 large spring roll wrappers (Blue Dragon,
   Vietnamese)
Sunflower oil for frying

1) First make the sauce: Mix all the ingredients together in a small serving bowl and set aside.
2) Make the filling for the spring rolls in a large bowl by mixing together the first 8 ingredients.
3) Take the roll wrappers out of the packet and fill a shallow baking tray with very hot water. Place a spring roll wrapper into it and leave it in until it is soft and pliable, about 20 seconds.
4) Remove the wrapper and lay it on the top half of a clean wet tea towel and blot with the bottom half until the wrapper is slightly sticky. Place a line of filling along the centre of the wrapper but not right to the edge. Then fold the bottom of the wrapper up over the filling, fold in the sides totally covering the filling and then roll the wrapper upwards to form a neat roll shape.
5) Repeat until they are all made but keep the water hot. Alternatively, deep fry them in sunflower oil for about 1 minute on each side or until crisp and golden. I suggest using a wok for this. Serve immediately with dipping sauce.

CARAMELIZED RED ONION TARTS

This is a lovely starter for a party or as a main course on a bed of rocket for a lunch. You can also make one large tart and serve it with a bowl of salad instead. The cheeses you use can vary, feta-style, mozzarella-style or if suitable a log of goats' or sheeps' cheese thickly sliced. Serves 6

Shortcrust pastry, see page 119
500g/1lb 2oz red onions, peeled, halved and finely sliced
2 tablespoons olive oil
1 teaspoon dried or 2 of fresh thyme leaves
2 tablespoons balsamic vinegar
2 teaspoons granulated sugar

Pinch of sea salt and freshly ground black pepper
120-170g/4-6oz tub Cheezly Greek-style dairy-free cheese cubes in oil, drained and cubed, or 1x log of goats'/ewes' cheese, thickly sliced (do not use any cream cheese as this will not melt)

•• Preheat oven to 180C/350F/Gas 4.
•• You will need a metal fluted 10cm/4in round pastry cutter and a 12-hole deep muffin tin/pan, baking parchment, ceramic baking beans or balls and gluten-free flour for dusting.

1) Make the pastry recipe on page 119 and during the pastry chilling time prepare the onions. Cook them gently in a large frying pan in the oil and thyme leaves until softened but not browned.
2) Add the vinegar, sugar and seasoning and cook until soft and melting to the taste. Reserve until needed.
3) Roll the pastry dough on a floured flat surface or board with a floured rolling pin until you think that you can cut out 12 circles. I normally manage about 8 and then need to re-roll the pastry and cut out 4 more.
4) Line the tins by gently pushing down the pastry so that no air is trapped. Prick the bottoms with a fork and line each one with a small circle of the baking parchment and some ceramic baking beans/balls.
5) Bake blind for about 15 minutes (see page 119). Carefully remove paper and balls onto a plate and return the tarts to the oven to cook the base. Allow about 5-10 minutes until golden and cooked through.
6) Fill the tarts with the onion mixture, top with the Greek-style cheese cubes or a thick slice of goats'/ewes' cheese and bake for about 10 minutes or until the pastry is golden and the cheese is melting. Serve immediately.

SMOKED SALMON AND DILL TARTS

You can make one large rectangular tart for parties or picnics, which somehow looks far more impressive than a large round one. I serve these tarts on a bed of wild rocket leaves with a drizzle of olive oil and a twist of black pepper. You can make them with shortcrust pastry (recipe page 119) if you do not have any puff pastry handy. Makes 12 tarts

500g/1lb 2oz Lovemore Free From gluten-
   free frozen puff pastry
Rice flour for dusting
5 medium eggs
3 tablespoons dairy-free soya single cream
1 teaspoon dried dill or double of freshly
   chopped dill

Freshly ground black pepper
100g/3^{1}/2oz smoked salmon, cut into bite
   size bits
Cayenne pepper

•• You will need a 12 x deep hole non-stick muffin tin/pan.
•• Preheat the oven to 200C/400F/Gas 6.

1) Defrost the pastry; make sure you leave it for 10 minutes at room temperature.
2) Sprinkle a clean surface with rice flour and dust the rolling pin. Roll out the pastry into a large thin rectangle. Using a fluted round pastry cutter (8cm/3in) cut out 12 pastry circles.
3) Line your tin with each circle of pastry pushing down gently but be careful not to break the pastry.
4) In a small bowl whisk 3 whole eggs and 2 egg yolks with a fork. Add the soya cream, dill and black pepper. Whisk in the chopped salmon and spoon the mixture into each pastry case.
5) Sprinkle lightly with cayenne pepper. Bake in the centre of the oven for about 20 minutes or until both the pastry and filling is puffy and golden. Serve warm and as suggested in the introductory note or cool on a wire rack and keep at room temperature until ready to serve.

•• To use up the remaining pastry you can make mince pies, jam tarts, cheese straws or a small pie top.

VEGETABLE DISHES AND SALADS

I am a great fan of farmers' and local markets for seasonal fresh vegetables and fruits but I am first to admit that the supermarkets have a huge array of vegetables, salads and fruits too. I try and avoid anything packaged and marked as having flown from far flung corners of the world but occasionally the lure of kiwi, pineapple and other such delights are too tempting to resist.

The most important thing is to keep buying small amounts of fresh produce frequently so that you eat it fresh and not days old. This is of course the advantage of shopping in a market, as the basket gets heavier you are less likely to stockpile.

Vegetables should look fresh and sprightly, a bit of earth clinging on to them is encouraging too. Most of all the skins should look smooth and firm, if you see wrinkles, bruises, discolouration, soft or mouldy patches then you should definitely seek further.

It makes good sense to buy locally and in season, the products will be tastier and cheaper. Try not to buy more than you need for the next few days and store in a cool place in a vegetable rack so that the air circulates around them. If you have bought packaged vegetables or fruit then always unpack immediately and let the fruit breathe.

Cooking vegetables when they are fresh requires the minimum of time and effort. Boiling is the most dramatic and you loose a lot of goodness and colour from the vegetables. Always cut vegetables into similar sizes or they won't cook evenly. Most vegetables should be cooked al dente which means that they should be tender but with a slight firmness in the middle. Always serve them immediately or if you are using them as part of a recipe then run cold water over them so that they stop cooking and retain their bright colour.

A few vegetables can be fried such as onions, mushrooms and courgettes or aubergines but generally I prefer griddling. You use less fat in the pan and achieve those deeply satisfying brown stripes across the vegetable flesh. You cannot really griddle copious amounts of vegetables not only because of the time factor but the smoke alarm scenario! Resist frequent turning of vegetables in a griddle pan – just turn them once when half way through cooking.

Roast vegetables are my favourite because you have no water to draw out the flavour; every ounce of taste is still there at the end of cooking. The high heat creates patches of caramelization which adds to the deliciousness. It is also easy in the oven, they just need to be stirred occasionally and you only have to wash up one large roasting pan. You can roast one type of vegetable for example, parsnips, sweet potatoes, butternut squash etc. or a more Mediterranean mix of halved tomatoes, peppers, aubergines and courgettes with onions. Quite often I just mix anything I have and it is always delicious as you will see in the pasta recipe on page 57. The main thing is to make sure that the vegetables, whatever they are, have similar cooking times and are of similar size. Roast in a high oven for best results, drizzled with plenty of olive oil, sprinkled liberally with seasoning, fresh rosemary or thyme and finely chopped garlic and even chillies. Serve them immediately for the ultimate vegetable dish.

Now we go onto salads as I do have a few in this book. Salads can be very diverse and are completely different from 20 years ago. A good salad is easy but sometimes I think that the temptation to throw in any old left-over can ruin a dish that should be simple and fresh with a dash of dressing to coat it. Whatever goes into the salad should be in perfect condition because even if the dressing is delicious it will not mask limp rocket or spinach leaves or even worse to my mind over-ripe tomatoes and wrinkly peppers! A salad is a palate clearing and healthy dish not a dustbin. We should treat all the vegetables we eat with the respect they deserve and by preparing them at the last minute they will retain their freshness and taste.

A good salad should be composed rather than thrown together even if it is simply lettuce with the contrast of peppery rocket or watercress and frisee for bitterness. Some salads use starchy vegetables like chopped cold potatoes or beans and lentils in which case you want to toss them with dressing whilst still warm and make sure the dressing is a little sharper. Even if you only have time to dress your salads with a splash of balsamic vinegar, a dash of olive oil and some salt and pepper this will still be nectar and so much better than anything you can buy in a bottle.

GRATIN DAUPHINOISE

This recipe has been a challenge to me for years, how on earth do you get a classic and creamy potato dish that is dairy-free? Well this time I feel that I have cracked it with a super-cheat addition of cornflour. I know this is not classical but it is the only way in 10 years of cooking that the dish has not curdled. The choice of potato also makes a huge difference because some are too waxy and some are tough on top. Desiree potatoes make the finest gratin because they remain separate yet absorb just enough liquid to bake perfectly. Serves 8

Dairy-free sunflower spread

1.4kg/3lb Desiree potatoes, peeled, any blemishes removed

500ml/18fl.oz/2 cups unsweetened dairy-free soya milk

250ml/9fl.oz/1 cup soya dairy-free single cream

2 garlic cloves, peeled and chopped

2 sprigs fresh thyme or sprinkling of dried thyme leaves

1/2 small onion, peeled and thickly sliced

1 heaped dessertspoon pure cornflour mixed to a smooth liquid with cold water

A little freshly grated nutmeg

Sea salt and freshly ground black pepper

Optional: Dairy-free Parmazano grated cheese replacer (see stockists), or either goats' or pecorino cheese

•• Preheat the oven to 180C/350F/Gas 5.
•• You will need an oven-to-table gratin dish no less than 25cm/10in square, 7cm/2¹/2 in deep.

1) Rub a large knob of sunflower spread all over the surface of the gratin dish. Thinly slice the potatoes into neat and even sizes with a very sharp knife. Lay the slices on a clean tea towel, pat dry and keep covered whilst you infuse the soya milk.

2) Pour the soya milk and cream into a saucepan. Add the garlic, thyme and onions. Gently heat the milk to boiling point, stir in the dissolved cornflour and cook gently until it has thickened slightly. Leave to stand for 10 minutes.

3) Remove from the heat, strain the liquid through a fine sieve into a large jug and stir in the nutmeg.

4) Layer half the potato slices around the gratin dish not being too fussy about appearances. Season with a little salt and pepper as you go along but make the top layer tidier.

5) Pour over the milk mixture, sprinkle with the Parmazano if using and dot with plenty of knobs of sunflower spread.

6) Bake for about 1-1¹/2 hours, the top should be golden and crispy and the potatoes soft and creamy. Leave the dish to stand for 10 minutes before eating. Cooking time depends on how thickly you have sliced the potatoes and how big your dish is.

CAULIFLOWER WITH AROMATIC CRUMBS

I have taken this idea from a famous French dish but for me it needed jazzing up with a bit more flavour so that I could serve the cauliflower with roast lamb, pork or beef. In winter we like to have this dish with baked potatoes for lunch. Serves 4-6

50g/2oz tin anchovy fillets in olive oil, drained and chopped

2 heaped teaspoons fresh thyme leaves

2 heaped teaspoons freshly chopped rosemary leaves

4 heaped tablespoons freshly chopped parsley leaves

Zest of 1 large unwaxed lemon

5 tablespoons sunflower oil and olive oil for drizzling

5 cloves garlic, peeled and chopped

Freshly ground black pepper

2 very thick slices gluten-free white bread (see stockists)

1 large cauliflower, trimmed and leaves removed

•• Preheat the oven to 180C/350F/Gas 4.

1) Put the first 8 ingredients for the aromatic crumbs together in the food processor.

2) Cut off the crusts from the bread, cut the bread into cubes, add to the other ingredients and process until the mixture resembles breadcrumbs.

3) Cook the whole cauliflower in boiling water or steam it until al dente. If it is too soft it will fall to pieces. Carefully lift the cauliflower into a warm ovenproof serving dish.

4) Drizzle around the sides of the cauliflower with olive oil so that it doesn't dry out. Pat the crumb mixture onto the top of the cauliflower and bake in the oven for 35 minutes or until the crumbs are golden and crispy. Serve hot.

GRIDDLED COURGETTES AND MINT SALAD

A griddle is an excellent way of cooking lower fat food. If you don't already have one then I suggest investing in a large one so that you can cook for 4 people. Always heat the griddle until very hot before you start cooking and don't pour oil on the griddle but oil the food lightly instead. Serves 4-6

4 medium or large and firm courgettes
Sea salt and freshly ground black pepper
Olive oil
120-175g/4-6oz tub The Redwood Co.
   Cheezly Greek-style dairy-free cheese,

drained and roughly chopped or either
   goats' or pecorino cheese
4 heaped tablespoons chopped fresh mint
   leaves

1) Slice the courgettes thinly lengthwise and sprinkle with salt. This makes them sweat and gets rid of excess water. Leave the courgettes for 15 minutes and then rinse off with cold running water and pat dry with kitchen paper.
2) Heat the griddle until very hot, brush the courgettes with oil and griddle until charred lines are visible on both sides and the vegetables are just cooked through.
3) Arrange the courgettes on a serving dish, season with salt and pepper, drizzle with plenty of oil, scatter with the cheese and mint leaves and toss to combine. Serve or cover and keep cool until needed.

BRAISED FENNEL WITH CHILLI, LEMON AND THYME

This recipe is excellent with fish, chicken and pork and the delicate flavour of fennel is a contrast to the simplicity of steamed, poached or roast dishes. In the summer, the fennel becomes a delicious salad – simply leave it to chill. Bring it to room temperature and sprinkle with extra parsley and olive oil. Serves 6

3 tablespoons olive oil
4 large fennel, quartered (tops trimmed and
   discarded)
2 thyme sprigs
2 large cloves garlic, finely chopped
1 teaspoon coriander seeds and 1 teaspoon
   fennel seeds, toasted in a baking tray in a

hot oven for a few minutes
Small glass dry white wine
1 mild red chilli, halved, deseeded and
   finely chopped
Juice 1 large lemon
3 heaped tablespoons freshly chopped
   parsley leaves

1) Heat the oil in a very large frying pan and sauté the fennel for 5 minutes until it starts to brown. Turn the quarters over and sauté for another 5 minutes. Stir in the thyme, garlic, coriander and fennel seeds and the wine.
2) Reduce the heat and cook the fennel gently for about 25 minutes or until the fennel is al dente but tender. I suggest turning the quarters half way through cooking time.
3) Sprinkle over the chilli, lemon juice and scatter with parsley. Transfer to a warm dish to serve.

Butter and other fats

Butter and other fats can be used to start making your sauce as in a white sauce or to finish a sauce as in hollandaise sauce.

The butter makes a sauce taste creamy and rich but with margarine and dairy-free spreads the effect is far less marked. For extra creaminess more butter or fats are added which makes the texture of the sauce seem smoother too. Alternatively, goats' cream and dairy-free cream (soya) can be used to make the sauce richer and smoother. As long as there is enough flour in the sauce the fats/creams should not separate.

Flour and gluten-free flour

Flour is used as a base in all sauces derived from a white sauce such as béchamel sauce, cheese sauce, parsley sauce and others. The flour thickens any liquid that is used to make the sauce. The tiny granules of starch of any flour burst at boiling point when they are wet and hot. These granules collapse and spread becoming gelatinous and thickening the sauce as it is beaten or whisked.

Cornflour however, is a pure starch and although it thickens a sauce beautifully and quickly without having to make a roux, it doesn't make sauce with character or creaminess. It is perfect for thickening custard and making sure it doesn't curdle and a light gravy or stroganoff sauce.

A roux is the term used for the combination of melted butter or fat and an equal quantity of flour. The liquid is then worked in to make the sauce.

Liquids

The liquid base can be savoury, sweet or alcoholic! Chicken or vegetable stock can be used for sauces that cover vegetables or as part of a lasagne. A combination of stock with dairy-free milk is often used too. Sherries, wines, port and cider are all excellent ingredients for a sauce or gravy.

It doesn't usually matter whether the liquid is cold, hot or room temperature so don't worry about it unless the recipe is specific.

KEEPING SAUCES WARM

The only way to keep a sauce warm is to reheat it gently. Both gravy and butterscotch sauce can be reheated in its pan at the time of serving.

Other sauces can be treated in several ways:

- Transfer the finished sauce to a bowl and place a layer of cling film over the sauce. The cling film must stick to the surface of the sauce and this will prevent a skin forming. To reheat the sauce, remove cling film, turn the sauce into a clean pan and reheat gently stirring frequently.

- To reheat a delicate sauce that might either curdle or become granular like a chocolate or hollandaise sauce simply transfer the sauce into a heatproof bowl and set in a slightly larger bowl of very hot water. This provides all-round heat and will warm through or melt the sauce to the correct consistency. Stir regularly so that the sauce in the bottom of the bowl doesn't overheat.

- To reheat a less delicate sauce transfer it to a clean small bowl and set it over a pan with simmering water in it. Make sure the water doesn't come into contact with the sauce bowl and stir frequently until warm through and the correct consistency.

BASIC WHITE SAUCE

The art of a good white sauce is that it should coat the main ingredient of the dish, it should be thick enough to stay on the food, but it should not be so thick that it masks the contours and colour beneath it.

White sauce if it is not cooked enough has a raw flour flavour which isn't very nice so this is the one sauce that needs to come to boiling point and then cook through over lower heat. This ensures that the granules have burst and mixed into the sauce.

This is a basic white sauce which can be transformed into a béchamel sauce by infusing the milk beforehand for about 30 minutes. This is well worth doing if you have time because it makes up for the lack of flavour in the soya or other dairy-free milks.

INFUSION

1/2 carrot, peeled
1/2 small onion, peeled
5cm/2in piece of celery
10 whole black peppercorns

3 stalks of parsley tied together with a bit
    of kitchen string
1 bay leaf

1) Place all the ingredients in the pan with the milk and bring to the boil slowly. Remove from the heat and leave. Strain into a jug and then follow the white sauce recipe.

WHITE SAUCE

Makes 570ml/1 pint

55g/2oz dairy-free sunflower spread
45g /11/2 oz/heaped 1/3 cup Doves Farm
    gluten-free plain flour, sifted

570ml/1pint/2 cups + 2 tablespoons
    unsweetened dairy-free soya milk
Sea salt and freshly ground black pepper

•• You will need a medium sized balloon whisk.

1) Melt the sunflower spread over low heat in a medium sized heavy-based pan. It must not brown or it will affect the flavour and colour of the sauce.
2) Remove from the heat and stir in the flour with a wooden spoon until you have a smooth paste.
3) Return the pan to the heat and gradually pour in the soya milk a little at a time, about 55ml/2fl.oz will do, and whisking with a balloon whisk until the liquid is incorporated into the flour mix. If you whisk thoroughly before each liquid addition the sauce will not become lumpy unless the heat is too high. If it does become lumpy then simply sieve the end product or liquidise it.
4) Whisk until the sauce is smooth and glossy, cook through for about 5 minutes, and season to taste. Use in your recipe as instructed. Loosen with a little extra milk if it is thicker than you require.

CHEESE SAUCE

This is a basic cheese sauce; it is perfect for making cauliflower cheese and other vegetable dishes. Macaroni cheese (pictured opposite), lasagne, egg, fish or chicken dishes are also made with cheese sauce. It freezes well as part of any of these dishes although personally I find that eggs become too rubbery to bother. Makes 570ml/1 pint

55g/2oz dairy-free sunflower spread
40g/1^{1}/2 oz/^{1}/3 cup Doves Farm gluten-
  free plain flour
570ml/1 pint/2 cups + 2 tablespoons
  unsweetened dairy-free soya milk
Sea salt and freshly ground black pepper
A pinch of mustard powder
A pinch of cayenne pepper

1 teaspoon Life Free From gluten-free
  Worcester sauce
1 heaped tablespoon dairy-free Parmazano
  cheese (see stockists) or plenty of goats'
  or pecorino cheese
55g/2oz ready-grated or sliced dairy-free
  hard cheese (see stockists) or either
  goats' or pecorino cheese

•• You will need a medium sized balloon whisk.

1) Melt the sunflower spread over medium-low heat in a medium sized heavy-based pan. It must not brown or it will affect the flavour and colour of the sauce.
2) Remove from the heat and stir in the flour until you have a smooth paste.
3) Return the pan to the heat and gradually pour in the soya milk a little at a time, about 25ml/1fl.oz will do, and whisking with a balloon whisk until the liquid is incorporated into the flour. If you beat thoroughly before each liquid addition the sauce will not become lumpy unless the heat is too high. If it does become lumpy then simply sieve the end product or liquidise it.
4) Whisk until the sauce is smooth and glossy, bring to simmer point and cook through for about 3 minutes.
5) Beat or whisk in the mustard powder, cayenne, pepper, Worcester sauce, Parmazano, grated or diced hard cheese and stir until the sauce is smooth again. Adjust the seasoning, other flavours and even the cheeses according to your taste.

GRAVY

Gravy is made from the fat and the juices which come from the roasting joint or chicken. As we all have smaller joints nowadays we need to use these juices as a base for our sauce rather than as the sauce. Commercially made gravies will all have unsuitable starches in, even if you can find gluten-free alternatives the chemical additives will not enhance your delicious roast. In order to make a dependable gravy it is best to start at the beginning when you are about to roast the meat or bird. Allow a small onion and carrot for a small roast and large ones for a big roast. Place the roughly chopped onions and carrots with a couple of bay leaves, few sprigs of thyme or rosemary, some chopped garlic (with lamb, pork and chicken) and a glass of red wine for meat and white wine for fowl. Cider is good with chicken, pheasant and pork and port or sherry is also good with beef. Allow a small but full wine glass for a small roast and a large one for a bigger roast. Place the meat or fowl on top, brush with oil, sprinkle with seasoning and herbs if suitable. Pour a glass of water around the roast and cook in the oven according to the recipe.

Here are two ways to make gravy.
1) This method makes a small amount of thin gravy.
   - Remove the roast meat or fowl from the pan and leave it to rest on a carving board or plate whilst you make the gravy.
   - Take the roasting pan of juices and with a spoon discard most of the fat from the juices. Return the pan to the medium heat. Use a wooden spoon to scrape all the crusty bits around the pan and back into the juices. This is deglazing.
   - Add a small glass of stock or vegetable water and bring to the boil, stir and simmer for about 5 minutes. Add a couple of tablespoons of port, sherry or cider, if you like at this point. Simmer for a couple of minutes, adjust the seasoning and pour into a warm gravy boat or jug.
2) This next method makes thicker gravy for a larger quantity. Deal with the meat, game or fowl as before.
   - **Make a roux:** Mix double the amount of gluten-free flour to dairy-free spread and beat until smooth paste. To make gravy for about 8-10 people I suggest one heaped tablespoon of dairy-free spread to 2 of gluten-free flour and you may have some roux left or you may need some more. Once you have cooked a few roasts and put in roughly the same amount of base ingredients into your pan to start with you will be able to judge just by looking at the pan.
   - Carefully hold the roasting pan of juices and tipping it forward spoon out most of the fat leaving the juices. Use a wooden spoon to scrape all the crusty bits around the pan back into the juices.
   - Add one full large wine glass of stock or vegetable water to the juices in the roasting pan, place on top of medium heat and bring to the boil. Let it bubble for about 10 minutes stirring occasionally. Pour the gravy through a sieve to catch any vegetables, discard them and return the gravy to the pan. At this point you can add a couple of tablespoons of port, sherry or cider.
   - Whisk in half of the roux with a balloon whisk and keep beating it into the simmering juices. Work quickly or the flour will set into lumps! Repeat until the sauce reaches the desired thickness and is glossy and rich to the taste. Adjust the seasoning and serve in a warm jug or gravy boat.
- •• To make this for a small roast simply reduce the proportions to about 1 dessertspoon of dairy-

free sunflower spread to 2 spoons of gluten–free flour mix.
- •• For roast lamb you can stir in a tablespoon of redcurrant jelly to the finished gravy. For beef, game and fowl a handful of wild or cultivated sliced mushrooms at the start give a richer and more intense flavour. A handful of peeled and sliced apples added at the start of cooking can sweeten and lift for pork or pheasant gravy.

BREAD SAUCE

Bread sauce is a wonderfully English concoction to accompany roast chicken, turkey or pheasant. You can't make it with brown bread and so you need a really good gluten-free white loaf. Usually the longer-life the loaf the worse it tastes so try and find a loaf with a week shelf-life. Here it is vital to flavour the milk with an infusion as you have very little flavour from the loaf compared to a classic white loaf. If you are also using soya milk then the infusion should be a little stronger and by adding the soya cream and a knob of dairy-free spread the sauce at last becomes convincingly delicious. Serves 6

1 small onion studded with 8 cloves
500ml/18fl.oz/2 cups unsweetened dairy-
   free soya milk
2 bay leaves
1 sprig of thyme
8 black peppercorns

100g/3^1/$_2$oz/2 cups freshly made gluten-
   free white breadcrumbs (see stockists)
30g/1oz dairy-free sunflower spread
Sea salt and freshly ground black pepper
2 tablespoons dairy-free soya single cream
A pinch of freshly grated nutmeg

- •• A few hours before making the sauce, infuse the milk.

1) To do this; cut the onion in half and stud each domed half with an equal amount of cloves.
2) Place the milk with the onions, clove side down, in a pan over medium heat and add the bay leaves, thyme and peppercorns.
3) Bring to the boil and then remove from the heat and leave to infuse for 2 hours or more.
4) Put the breadcrumbs into a medium sized pan, pour in the milk through a fine sieve and discard the additions. Stir in the sunflower spread, salt and pepper and cook very gently for about 5 minutes stirring frequently. Do not boil the sauce.
5) When the sauce is thick and creamy, stir in the cream and grated nutmeg and serve warm with the roast. Alternatively, reheat the sauce later with a little extra soya cream or milk.

ROCKET PESTO

This pesto is now widely available in stores selling fresh pasta but not in dairy-free form. It also makes a delicious dressing for a warm beef salad. Stir a few tablespoons of pesto into your salad dressing or swirl into soups or dips.

55g/2oz/1/3 cup pine nuts
55g/2oz fresh wild rocket, stalks included
1 garlic clove, peeled and coarsely chopped
55g/2oz Parmazano, dairy-free cheese
   replacer (see stockists) or either finely
   grated goats' or pecorino cheese

1 tablespoon fresh lemon juice
10 tablespoons olive oil plus extra
Sea salt and freshly ground black pepper

1) Place the pesto ingredients in a food processor and whiz briefly until the sauce is smooth.
2) Do not over-blend or you will have a purée and also ruin the nutty texture. Scrape the mixture into a serving bowl or jug and then stir in as much olive oil as you need to achieve a perfect consistency.
3) Store in an air-tight jar or container in the refrigerator until needed but use at room temperature.

CHOCOLATE SAUCE

The great thing about chocolate sauce is that it can be made in advance and heated up. The sauce can also be made with water, but the half milk with cream mix makes the sauce more dense and rich. This sauce will coat profiteroles or poached pears perfectly or is simply a divine topping for ice cream. Serves 4-6

175g/6oz Kinnerton Luxury Dark Chocolate, broken into squares
30g/1oz cocoa powder (dairy-free)
175g/6oz/scant cup caster sugar

310ml/11fl.oz/1¼ cups half and half mix of dairy-free unsweetened soya milk with dairy-free soya single cream

1) Put all the ingredients into a saucepan and stir over a low heat until the sugar and chocolate have completely dissolved.
2) Raise the heat and bring the mixture to the boil, then reduce the heat again and simmer for about 6 minutes. Keep stirring from time to time.
3) Pour into a jug to serve.

BUTTERSCOTCH SAUCE

This is a lovely buttery sauce; it is combined with sugar and cream to make a rich caramel flavour and is very sweet and sticky. There is a simple trick for measuring golden syrup. Hold a tablespoon in boiling water, quickly scoop out the syrup and it should just slide off the spoon into the pan. Repeat each time you need another spoonful. Serves 6

130g/4½oz/1 cup light muscovado sugar
2 heaped tablespoons of golden syrup
55g/2oz dairy-free sunflower spread

150ml/¼ pint/⅔ cup soya dairy-free single cream
Few drops pure vanilla extract

•• Use a 20cm/8in thick-based saucepan or the sugar will be too thick to melt.

1) Put all the sugar into a saucepan. Bash out any hard lumps of sugar so that it cooks evenly. I use a potato masher! Stir over medium heat until the sugar is dissolved and creamy.
2) Increase the heat and stirring frequently let the sugar streak with caramel until it bubbles up into melted caramel bubbles. Maybe a few seconds of bubbles will be enough. The more you boil the sugar the more the sauce will taste of burnt caramel. Proceed cautiously – you can always make it more caramelized next time. Practise will perfect the timing of this sauce!
3) Quickly remove the pan from the heat and beat in the syrup and sunflower spread. Return the pan to the heat and bring the mixture up to the boil, stirring all the time, let the sauce boil for a couple of minutes only.
4) Remove the pan from the heat and gradually stir in all the soya cream and the vanilla. Keep stirring until well combined, smooth and glossy.
5) Serve warm or cold. You can keep it in a screw-top jar for a few days in a cool place.

PANCAKES AND BATTER

Pancakes exist in one form or another all over the world. In Russia they are called blinis and served with soured cream and caviar. The French love their crêpes which can be savoury or sweet and found in little crêperies all over the country. Pancakes are cheap and once you have mastered the art of making a thin pancake which you can successfully toss and cook evenly they are a Godsend for entertaining.

What is really important is using the right pan. You need a good heavy-based frying pan not more than 18cm/7in in diameter. If you use a larger pan the batter is harder to distribute evenly and you get ragged edges. It is essential that the pan is hot and lightly greased. If there is too much fat the pancakes will be heavy and soggy. You only need enough fat to prevent the pancakes from sticking not to fry them.

Pancakes can either be eaten immediately or they can be stored in the refrigerator or freezer for later use. For use within 24 hours simply lay a piece of greaseproof paper on a flat plate, place a cooked pancake on top and repeat the layers of paper and pancakes until they are all piled up. Allow to come to room temperature and then add a final layer of baking parchment on the top. Wrap in cling film and refrigerate. Reheat the stack by removing the cling film and replacing with foil and leaving in a warm oven for about 10 minutes to refresh them before following your recipe.

For freezing just place the pancakes on a freeze-proof dish and follow the above. Defrost a few hours before needed and follow the warming instructions before tackling the recipe.

BASIC PANCAKE BATTER

This is the batter I have used throughout my cooking career, it is light and doesn't need to stand and makes nice thin pancakes that come out of the pan easily. They can be kept for a day or frozen and re-heated. Makes 10-12 small pancakes

115g/4oz/3/4 cup Doves Farm gluten-free
    plain flour
A pinch of sea salt
2 large eggs

275ml/1/2 pint/1 cup + 2 tablespoons
    unsweetened dairy-free soya milk
2 tablespoons melted dairy-free sunflower
    spread
Sunflower oil for cooking the pancakes

•• You will also need a 20cm/8in non-stick frying pan, greaseproof paper and palette knife.

1) Sift the flour and salt into a big bowl; hold the sieve high to give the flour plenty of air.
2) Make a well in the centre of the flour and break the eggs into it.
3) Now start to whisk the eggs with a hand whisk, incorporating the flour gradually. Once you have a thick paste but still some flour remaining then start to add small quantities of soya milk, ignoring the lumps which will disappear.
4) Use a spatula to bring down any remaining bits of flour from the sides of the bowl and then give the batter a good whisk until it is smooth and the consistency of thin cream.
5) Transfer the mixture to a pouring jug. Lightly brush your palette knife and pan with oil.
6) Add 2 tablespoons of melted sunflower spread to the batter just before making the pancakes and whisk it in. Stir the batter every time you use it.
7) Let the pan get really hot over high heat, turn the heat down a fraction, lift the pan off the heat and with the other hand pour in enough batter to swirl around the pan very thinly and evenly. Return to the heat immediately.
8) A good tip is to pour smaller amounts of the batter into an easy pouring jug or simply to use a couple of tablespoons of the batter each time. The pancake should cook very quickly so make sure it doesn't have any burn spots on it. The pancakes should be pale gold in colour.
9) Use a palette knife to lift up the edge of the pancake and see if it is tinged with golden brown. Then flip it over and cook on the other side for the same amount of time. As the pancake is wafer thin it is easier to gently slide it out of the pan onto a flat warm dish lined with non-stick baking paper.
10) Keep making the pancakes and layer them with small sheets of the paper. They will keep warm so that you can all eat them together or you can leave them to cool. Wrap in cling film and keep cool until needed or freeze them. To reheat simply re-cook in a little oil, toss, fill and serve!

For lemon pancakes: sprinkle each one with lemon juice and caster sugar, fold in half and half again to form triangles.
For jam pancakes: warm some jam in a small pan, put a dessertspoonful in the middle of each pancake, and roll up by folding the ends inwards like a parcel and serve.

BLINIS WITH SMOKED SALMON AND CREAMED CHEESE

Home-made blinis taste and feel completely different from the rubbery tasteless packs in the chiller cabinet of various superstores. These are light and fluffy and a gentle foil for some exotic topping. As yet I have not found a gluten-free version for sale anywhere. You can make heaps of mini blinis as canapés and you can use either smoked salmon or smoked trout as the topping. Serves 4-6

Blinis
55g/2oz/generous 1/2 cup buckwheat flour
55g/2oz/generous 1/2 cup Doves farm gluten-free plain flour
1 teaspoon gluten-free baking powder
1 teaspoon olive oil
2 tablespoons sunflower oil
2 eggs, beaten
120ml/4fl.oz/1/2 cup water
A drop of extra oil for frying

Topping
225g/8oz tub Tofutti Creamy Smooth original soya cream cheese-style dip, (see stockists) or soft goats'/ewes' cheese
1 tablespoon unsweetened dairy-free soya milk
155g/51/2oz good quality smoked salmon or trout, cut into small strips
25g/1oz fresh chives, trimmed and then finely chopped

•• Optional decoration, fresh dill or rocket leaves.

1) Sift the flours with the baking powder into a bowl, make a well in the centre and pour in the oils and eggs.
2) Stir with a balloon whisk or fork and gradually incorporate the water.
3) Leave the batter to stand at room temperature for 15 minutes.
4) Heat a large non-stick frying pan with a drop of extra oil until very hot.
5) Pour a tablespoonful of the blini mixture into the pan and repeat until you have 4 blinis, each about 6cm/21/2in diameter. Keep repeating this format until you have enough blinis.
6) Cook the blinis until they are firm on the underside and bubbling on the upper side, then turn them over and cook the other side. Both sides should be pale gold.
7) Transfer the blinis onto a large warm serving plate.
8) Mix the dairy-free dip with the soya milk in a small bowl and beat until smooth. Place a blob onto the centre of each blini.
9) Arrange the salmon or trout on top and sprinkle with chives. Serve immediately, or transfer enough blinis per person onto smaller warm plates and decorate with little whisps of fresh dill, or rocket leaves with a drizzle of olive oil.

AMERICAN PANCAKES WITH MAPLE SYRUP

These pancakes are much thicker than English pancakes or French crêpes. They are served in a stack with melted butter and maple syrup and perk up a winter's breakfast with crispy bacon. Makes about 10

260ml/9fl.oz/1 cup unsweetened dairy-free soya milk
2 medium eggs
75g/3oz melted dairy-free sunflower spread
Grated zest 1 unwaxed orange
A few drops pure vanilla extract
1 1/2 tablespoons caster sugar

55g/2oz/1/2 cup Doves Farm gluten-free plain flour
200g/7oz/1 1/2 cups Doves Farm gluten-free self raising flour
A little oil
Extra dairy-free sunflower spread
Maple syrup to serve

1) With a balloon whisk, whisk the milk, eggs, melted sunflower spread, zest and vanilla in a large bowl. Whisk in the sugar, followed by both flours.
2) Whisk the batter until smooth. Oil the palette knife and repeat this throughout.
3) Brush the base of the pan with a little oil and then heat the pan until hot. Turn down the heat to medium.
4) Pour in a spoonful of batter, using a large serving spoon and make a circle of about 10cm/4in in diameter.
5) Make enough to fill the pan but ensure that the pancakes are not touching each other.
6) Cook for about 40 seconds on each side or until bubbling and golden. Continue the process of greasing and cooking.
7) Place the pancakes on a warm plate until they are all made.
8) Melt some sunflower spread over low heat and pour into a warmed jug.
9) Serve the pancakes in stacks with the melted spread and maple syrup poured over or close at hand. Alternatively, serve with dairy-free vanilla ice cream and maple syrup.

SCOTCH PANCAKES

You can make these pancakes, or drop scones as they are also called, in a few minutes. They must then be cooked straight away and eaten immediately. The vanilla extract disguises the slightly different taste that the flour has versus traditional wheat flour. Use a thick-based pan to prevent burning. Makes 15

115g/4oz/scant cup Orgran self raising flour
2 level tablespoons caster sugar
1 large egg, beaten & mixed with 1 teaspoon pure vanilla extract

150ml/1/4 pint/1/2 cup unsweetened dairy-free soya milk
Sunflower oil for greasing
Dairy-free sunflower spread and honey for serving

1) Put the flour and sugar into a bowl. Make a well in the centre and pour in the beaten egg and vanilla mixture.
2) Whisk the ingredients together, gradually incorporating the milk until it is smooth and shiny. Pour the thick batter into a jug.
3) Heat a frying pan over medium heat and grease by brushing oil with a pastry brush. When it is hot but not smoking pour in 3 circles of the batter (about 5cm/2in) and cook the pancakes in batches until all the batter is used up.
4) Cook each pancake for about 1 minute on one side and when bubbles form on top of the pancake and the underside is golden, flip it over with an oiled palette knife and cook the other side for 1 minute.
5) Hand them over to hungry mouths as you make them and quickly spread with sunflower spread. Honey is delicious on these pancakes.

APPLE PANCAKES
WITH BUTTERSCOTCH SAUCE

In the autumn when we can pick blackberries, I love pancakes filled with stewed apples and blackberries served with vanilla dairy-free ice cream. Otherwise we have poached pears or apples, both of which go extremely well with the sauce. If you don't have time to make the sauce then buy a good maple syrup and serve that instead. Serves 6

Butterscotch Sauce recipe page 47
Filling
8 large eating apples, peeled, quartered
   and cored

Juice of half large lemon
Pancakes recipe page 49
Swedish Glace dairy-free vanilla ice cream
   to serve

1) Make the butterscotch sauce as instructed and reserve or gently reheat the sauce if it was made in advance.
2) Roughly chop the apples and gently cook in a pan with the lemon juice and just enough water to stop the fruit drying out or sticking to the base of the pan. Stir occasionally over medium heat until you have a lumpy purée. Turn off the heat and keep the apple warm.
3) Make 12 small pancakes 14cm/5^1/2in diameter stacking them on a warm plate as you go.
4) When all the pancakes are made spread one at a time with a layer of the warm purée. Roll each pancake into a neat roll and serve two pancakes per person on a warm plate.
5) Drizzle with butterscotch sauce and serve with the vanilla ice cream. Eat immediately!

MACARONI CHEESE

A few years ago I came across a good gluten-free macaroni by Orgran and at last we could have macaroni cheese again (picture on page 43). It is the best comfort food on a cold day and by adding tomatoes on top the children get a veggie portion too! Serves 4-6

Cheese Sauce x 570ml/1 pint recipe
  page 42
250g/8¹/2oz pack Orgran rice and corn
  gluten-free macaroni
A few ripe vine tomatoes, skinned and
  sliced thickly

4 slices Tofutti Creamy Smooth dairy-free
  mozzarella-style slices or either finely
  grated goats' or pecorino cheese
Paprika or cayenne pepper

•• You will need a deep oven-to-table dish about 25cmx6.5cm/10x2^1/2in.
•• Preheat the grill whilst arranging the topping.

1) Make the cheese sauce.
2) While the sauce is cooking through bring a large pan of water to the boil. Add the pasta and cook until al dente.
3) Drain and rinse the pasta under hot running water in a colander. Transfer the pasta to the dish and shake until evenly distributed.
4) Pour over the warm cheese sauce and gently combine. Arrange the sliced tomatoes in a line down the centre of the dish. Cover with the slices of mozzarella-style cheese or the grated cheese. Lightly sprinkle with paprika or cayenne (not for younger children) and cook under the grill until melted and bubbling. Serve immediately.

FUSILLI WITH ROASTED VEGETABLES AND OLIVES

This easy pasta dish can be served hot or cold so you can adapt it to seasonal vegetables and serve any time of the year. Personally I prefer to serve pasta dishes without the accompaniment of dairy-free grated cheese. However, goats' or pecorino cheese is fine to use if you would like to. Serves 4-6

100g/3^1/2oz trimmed asparagus tips
1 yellow pepper and 1 red pepper, seeded and chopped into quarters
2 medium red onions cut into 8 wedges each
3 medium courgettes cut into bite size diagonal chunks
4-6 large vine tomatoes, stalks and tops sliced off
Plenty of olive oil for roasting and tossing
2 large garlic cloves, crushed

1 sprig rosemary leaves finely chopped
A medium chilli, deseeded and finely chopped
Sea salt and freshly ground black pepper
85g/3oz/^{1}/2 cup pitted black olives in oil, drained
255g/9oz pack gluten-free fusilli pasta
Zest and juice of 1 unwaxed large lemon
30g/1oz fresh flat-leaf parsley, finely chopped

•• Preheat the oven to 200C/400F/Gas 6.

1) Blanch the asparagus in a pan of simmering water over medium heat for 3 minutes, then drain in a colander and keep to one side.
2) Place all the vegetables in a large roasting pan, and sprinkle with plenty of olive oil, the garlic, rosemary and chopped chilli. Season with salt and pepper and toss them around to make sure everything is evenly coated.
3) Roast the vegetables in the oven for about 1^1/2 hours or until all the vegetables are cooked – some will be browned or crispy at the edges and some will just be softly cooked and glazed. Half way through cooking time, remove the pan from the oven and add the olives and asparagus and gently shake the pan so that they are evenly distributed.
4) About 20 minutes before the end of cooking time, bring a pan of water to the boil.
5) Cook the pasta according to the instructions until al dente.
6) Drain the pasta, transfer to a serving bowl and toss lightly with some olive oil. Season the pasta with a little salt and pepper and mix in the lemon zest and juice.
7) As soon as the vegetables are ready, mix them into the pasta, sprinkle with fresh parsley and serve.

Alternatively, wait for the mixture to cool, cover and chill until needed, but serve at room temperature.

CHEATING SPAGHETTI WITH MUSSELS

Spaghetti alle Vongole is one of my favourite pasta dishes but I haven't been able to find clams so I have simply changed the recipe to frozen mussels. No rinsing to get rid of any grit or discarding broken or damaged shells. These frozen mussels are ready to cook. You could also use cooked vacuum-packed ones or cook shell-on mussels as long as you have the same quantity of mussel meat. Serves 6

500g/1lb 2oz gluten-free spaghetti
4 tablespoons olive oil
2 large cloves garlic, finely chopped
Very finely chopped fresh chilli, as little
  or much as desired
400g/15oz can chopped tomatoes

1 small glass white wine
500g/1lb 2oz bag frozen cooked mussels
  (no shells)
Sea salt and freshly ground black pepper
2 heaped tablespoons chopped fresh parsley

1) Bring a pan of water to the boil for the pasta.
2) Cook the spaghetti until al dente in a large pan of boiling water.
3) Heat the oil in a large thick-based pan over medium heat, briefly cook the garlic and chilli for a few seconds and then stir in the tomatoes and wine.
4) Cook the mixture for about 10 minutes, add the mussels and then bring to simmering point and leave until the sauce and mussels are hot. Do not leave any longer or the mussels will become tough and leathery.
5) Season to taste with salt and pepper.
6) Drain the spaghetti and toss it in with the mussel mixture. Sprinkle with parsley and serve immediately.

VEGETARIAN LASAGNE

Lasagne is such a faff to prepare but we all love it and I usually divide this recipe into two dishes and freeze one for another day. This is delicious enough to be suitable for a dinner or lunch party if you have a vegetarian guest. The sauce should be light, sweet and full of flavour which will contrast nicely with the rich, deep flavour of the mushrooms. Serves 8

Cheese sauce, **double quantity of recipe page 42**

Tomato sauce
2 medium onions, finely chopped
2 tablespoons olive oil
3x400g/14oz cans chopped tomatoes in sauce
Sea salt and freshly ground black pepper
2 large garlic cloves, crushed
1 small mild chilli, halved, deseeded and chopped
2 bay leaves
2 heaped teaspoons fresh thyme leaves

Mushroom filling
500g/1lb 2oz large, flat chestnut or portobello mushrooms
500g/1lb 2oz courgettes, sliced
2 large leeks, trimmed, washed and sliced
25g/1oz packet dried mixed wild mushrooms
6 tablespoons olive oil
1 tablespoon fresh thyme leaves
1 large garlic clove, crushed
Sea salt and freshly ground black pepper
Sprinkling of freshly grated nutmeg

Lasagne
8-10 sheets gluten-free lasagne, (depending on the brand, they can vary in size)
1 packet of dairy-free mozzarella-style cheese slices or plenty of buffalo mozzarella, sliced or either goats' or pecorino cheese finely grated
Sprinkling of cayenne pepper

•• 33cm/13in long and 20cm/8in wide oven-to-table dish.
•• Preheat the oven to 190C/375F/Gas 5.

1) Make the cheese sauce first and set aside. Then make the tomato sauce; in a pan over low heat gently cook the onions until softened in the oil, do not brown them. Stir in the chopped tomatoes with all the remaining sauce ingredients.

2) Simmer the sauce for 25 minutes, stirring with a wooden spoon from time to time until it is a soft pulp. Adjust the seasoning and then leave the sauce to cool.

3) Make the mushroom filling; Peel and trim the fresh mushrooms, quarter them and slice them thinly. Sauté them with the courgettes, leeks and dried mushrooms in a big non-stick pan in the oil, over medium heat, until they have softened.

4) Stir in the thyme and garlic, make sure the vegetables are evenly coated with oil and cooked through. Season them with salt, pepper and grated nutmeg and leave to cool.

5) Spread half of the tomato sauce over the base of the baking dish. Cover the sauce with half the strips of lasagne – they can overlap each other but you don't want thick layers of stodgy pasta. You can break pieces to fit around the edges and corners.

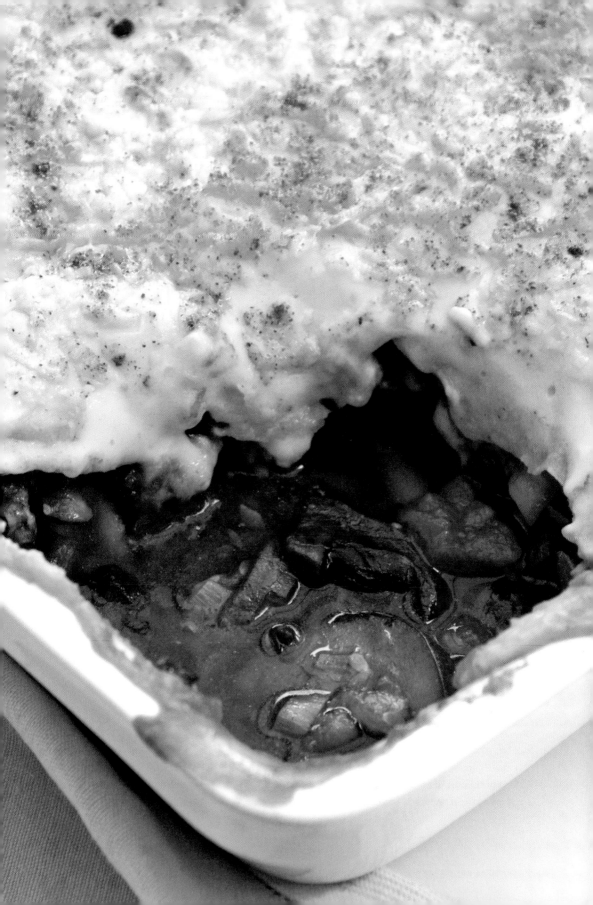

The second bout of kneading is much quicker because it is just distributing the air bubbles throughout the dough. Either way, when you bake the pizza the air bubbles expand in the heat of the oven to make a light bready texture.

Kneading is tough work but is rather therapeutic if you are feeling a bit stressed!

- Sprinkle the work surface with some gluten-free flour mix and onto the palms of your hands.

- Place the dough on the floured surface and push the heel of your right hand into the dough and then away from you. Use your other hand to steady the dough.

- You need to stretch the dough out, this naturally becomes easier as the gluten develops in the strong flour but not if it is a gluten-free mix. Fold the stretched bit of dough back over on to the rest of the dough, then turn the dough and repeat.

- You will eventually get a good rhythm going but might need a rest occasionally. Keep going for 5-10 minutes to ensure a stretchy but satin finish.

MOZZARELLA, PINE NUT AND ARTICHOKE PIZZA

You can add to the topping ingredients other favourites such as slices of chorizo, strips of cured ham or anchovies.

Personally I am not keen on some of the modern toppings, I like the traditional Italian toppings. I saw a pizza the other day which had not only the thinnest layer of tomato sauce on it but a rocket salad plonked on top with a few small shavings of Parmesan – why?! Makes 2 huge thin pizzas

Base
400g/14oz/3 generous cups Doves Farm gluten-free plain white flour
1 teaspoon sea salt
2 teaspoons unrefined golden caster sugar
14g/1$1/4$ teaspoons fast acting yeast (check it is gluten-free)
300ml/$1/2$ pint/1$1/4$ cups warm water
Extra gluten-free flour for dusting and kneading
Topping
$1/2$ x 200g/7oz jar Drossa caper berries, stalks removed (see stockists)
6 tablespoons of tomato purée
Half x 425g/15oz can artichoke hearts, drained
About 20 stoned black olives in oil, drained

$3/4$ x 260g/9oz tub of Cheezly Greek-style cheese cubes in oil, drained or either goats' or pecorino cheese in small cubes
2 heaped tablespoons pine nuts
2 tablespoons olive oil and extra for drizzling
Freshly ground black pepper
1 teaspoon dried or 2 of fresh oregano leaves
Light sprinkling of dried chilli flakes (according to taste)
100g/3$1/2$oz dairy-free mozzarella-style slices or rather more of buffalo mozzarella (see stockists) or either goats' or pecorino cheese, grated

•• Preheat the oven to 220C/425F/Gas 7.

•• You will need 2 pizza trays 30.5cm/12in in diameter.

1) Mix the flour, salt, sugar and yeast in a bowl. Make a well in the middle, mix in the water with floured hands and bring the mixture together. Flour the ball of dough and transfer to a floured board or surface.

2) Knead the dough for 8 minutes until it is elastic and pliable. Kneading is easy and great for getting rid of stress! Simply use your strongest hand to knead and your weaker side to keep the dough in the same area. Knead in a calm, firm rhythm. Bring the farthest end of the dough over and back towards you with your fingers and then knead with the base of your hand, repeat a few times and then turn and repeat. Keep going so that the dough is evenly kneaded.

3) If it is too sticky add a sprinkling more flour and if it is too dry add a sprinkling more water as explained above.

4) Lightly oil 2 bowls, divide the dough in half, score a cross in the top of each one with a knife and cover with cling film.

5) Leave to rise for 1–1 1/2 hours in a warm place. Meanwhile, rinse the caper berries in cold water and then leave in a bowl of cold water to reduce the saltiness. Drain them and pat dry with kitchen paper before using.

6) Take the dough and place on a floured board and knock each one back with your fist. Knead for a few minutes and flatten the dough with your hands.

7) Roll out the dough until you have two pizzas no more than 3mm/1/8in thick in the middle and a little thicker at the edge. Place on the baking sheets.

8) Spread the tomato purée all over the top of each pizza and quarter the artichokes.

9) Distribute the olives, artichokes, Greek-style cheese, caper berries and pine nuts all over the tomato.

10) Drizzle a little oil all over the top, season with some black pepper and sprinkle with oregano leaves and chilli flakes. Arrange the mozzarella slices or other cheese over the top and bake for about 15 minutes until golden around the edge and piping hot and serve immediately.

Here are some more topping suggestions

•• From stage 8, instead of artichokes, olives, caper berries and pine nuts, distribute about 100g/3 1/2oz sliced proscuitto or other allergy-free cured ham, shredded. A cup of finely sliced mushroom lightly cooked in olive oil.

•• From stage 8 distribute drained anchovies from a jar, drained roasted peppers in oil and a sprinkling of fried courgettes.

•• From stage 8 distribute fried slices of red onions in olive oil and thyme leaves, halved cherry tomatoes, fried thinly sliced chorizo (about 1/4 the 'U' shaped Spanish sausage).

For all three of the above toppings revert back to stage 10 to finish the pizza.

RICE

Rice is the staple diet for millions of people around the world but we tend to be more restrained in our consumption. Even so the shops are now stocking a huge variety of rice for us to try. Brown rice has more roughage than white and is always specified in diet books and magazine articles. It has a nice nutty flavour but not that melting and comforting texture. Rice in its natural state is a good source of proteins and vitamins essential to our health but of course much is lost during the polishing process. The good thing about rice is that it is really easily digested and so ideal for those with food intolerances. There are three sizes of grain and each one is suitable for a different type of dish.

Short-grain rice

This grain is often referred to as pudding rice in England; it is cheap because it grows so quickly. The grains are plump, almost round and rather chalky which makes them sticky and creamy when cooked. The rice is ideal for puddings.

Medium-grain rice

This grain is half-way between sticky when cooked like short-grain and cleanly separate like long-grain rice. It tends to be used for croquettes, rice moulds and some risottos.

Long-grain rice

The grain is long and narrow and without the chalkiness of the other grains it fluffs up and separates out when cooked. Good quality rice should have pointed ends and look fine, almost translucent.

- **Brown rice** is the whole natural grain of rice with only the inedible outer layer of husk removed so that the bran and germ are left intact. It comes in the above three sizes. Patna rice is the name often used for the long grain brown rice. It takes longer to cook but hangs on to the highest percentage of fibre, vitamins and minerals.

- **Easy-cook rice** is usually white and has been treated by a steaming process before milling. It takes about 10 minutes longer to cook than ordinary rice and is more expensive. It is supposed to help retain the nutritional content and to keep separate and less starchy during cooking.

- **Wild rice** is not strictly rice grain but a form of grass seed. It has a lovely nutty smoky flavour but it is expensive so I always suggest mixing it with long-grain brown rice. Cook the rice separately and mix them together with some dairy-free spread and freshly ground black pepper. This rice must not be overcooked or it goes mushy.

- **Basmati rice** is of very fine quality with a wonderful flavour and comes from India. I prefer this rice for serving with curries and spicy dishes. Brown basmati rice has even more flavour.

- **Arborio rice** from Italy is also fine quality rice. Its round, plump, chalkiness makes wonderful creamy risotto. It is not worth trying to make a risotto with other kinds of rice because they are not absorbent enough to take on all the flavours, fats and liquids.

- **Rice flakes** come from the grains which are broken during the milling process and make a very quick rice pudding. Ground rice is useful for thickening soups and rice puddings. It is also used in some baking recipes but the most useful rice product is rice flour. It is very diverse and can be used to make gluten-free pastry, cookies, cakes, puddings, bread and pasta as well as being a useful thickening agent. I also use it for making white or cheese sauces if I have run out of my gluten-free flour mix.

There are a few helpful tips about cooking rice and this should help you produce perfect rice each time.

- Don't wash rice because it has already been cleaned. You don't want to wash any more nutrients out! Cooking at high temperature will be quite enough.

- Always measure rice and liquid by volume not weight. A measuring jug is best. 150ml/5fl.oz is enough for two people with generous portions – just keep increasing the amount until you have enough. Then measure the liquid to twice the amount of rice e.g. 275ml/10fl.oz.

- Leave the rice whilst it is cooking, it is delicate and the grains break easily if prodded releasing the starch and turning the mixture sticky. Use a wide, shallow pan with a lid and turn the heat down once boiling point has been reached.

- Long-grain white rice takes 15 minutes to cook and brown rice about 40 minutes but in both cases all the water should be absorbed, if it isn't give it another few minutes.

- Test the rice is done by biting it, the rice should be tender but still firm. You can fluff up the rice just before serving.

- Try not to keep the rice warm for more than 20 minutes. Keep it in a warm dish covered with foil and leave in the oven at a very low temperature.

- Cooked rice keeps well in the refrigerator for 3-4 days as long as it is covered with cling film. It is useful for salads but can easily be reheated in a pan with a little water and shaken over the heat until warmed through.

RISOTTO

There are plenty of risotto recipes around but I am going to give you the classic base risotto to which you can add an endless variety and combination of ingredients once you are confident. My personal favourite is the classic Risotto Milanese – it is the simplest but to my mind the best recipe for any season.

Don't use cheap wines, it must be a decent white wine or the grains will take on a nasty taste. Use fresh/frozen stock but not from packets or cubes as it is too overpowering. Butter or dairy-free spread is used at the beginning to cook the onions and then at the end to finish off the risotto. Freshly grated Parmesan is used but you can use either grated pecorino or goats' cheese. For dairy-free I suggest Life Free From Parmazano which is the best alternative I can find and is easily available in supermarkets.

To cook the risotto:

- Melt the butter or dairy-free spread in a large shallow pan over low heat and then stir in the rice for a minute. This ensures that the grains are coated in the fat.

- Stir in a glass of white wine. This is one time when you do need to stir the grains as they cook. Once the wine is absorbed, add the stock a little at a time using a ladle. Stir regularly until half the liquid is absorbed.

- At this point add other ingredients such as a selection of uncooked tiny vegetables, seafood, chopped chicken or ham, roasted vegetable chunks, sun dried tomatoes, sliced mushrooms or spinach.

- Continue to cook, stir regularly and keep adding the stock until it is all used up and the added ingredients are either cooked or heated through as necessary.

- Add any fresh herbs. Chopped parsley or shredded basil are both delicious but sage or oregano can be used with tomatoes and stronger base flavours.

- If you like a gloopy type of risotto add more liquid but if you like a thick creamy one cook it for a bit longer and make sure all the liquid has been absorbed.

- Finish off the risotto by stirring in a generous knob of dairy-free spread, season to taste with salt and freshly ground black pepper and stir in the dairy-free Parmazano.

- Serve as soon as it has been cooked either as a starter or as a main course. If you try to keep the risotto hot it will go mushy and sticky.

Once you have mastered this simple risotto you can make up your own recipes and add whatever ingredient combinations you fancy such as chopped chicken or prawns or dried mushrooms. Do not use a heavy chardonnay or other very strong and oaked wines as they will overpower the subtle flavours.

RISOTTO PRIMAVERA

This is my simplest risotto, it is child friendly and you can add any left-over chopped ham or cooked chicken pieces. Serves 6

85g/3oz dairy-free sunflower spread
1 medium onion, finely chopped
200g/8oz baby broad beans
140g/5oz shelled or frozen peas
250g/9oz bunch fresh asparagus, trimmed
1 large clove garlic, finely chopped
350g/12oz Arborio or Carnaroli rice
1 glass of dry white wine

Sea salt and freshly ground black pepper
1.3 litres/2^1/$_4$ pints boiling chicken or
    vegetable stock
A large bunch of parsley, freshly chopped
Parmazano dairy-free grated cheese
    (see stockists) or either pecorino or
    goats' cheese

1) Melt the sunflower spread in a heavy-based saucepan.
2) Stir in the chopped onion and cook over low heat for 10 minutes until softened.
3) Meanwhile cook the broad beans in boiling water until al dente. Drain and refresh under cold running water. When the beans are cool enough, peel the skins off and discard. Cook the peas in boiling water, drain and reserve. Cook the asparagus until al dente, drain, cut into bite size lengths and reserve.
4) Stir the garlic and rice into the onions and cook for a minute before adding the wine and a little salt. Keep stirring the rice and add a little stock, stir the rice regularly adding a little more liquid each time it has been absorbed.
5) As soon as the rice is cooked and all the stock is absorbed remove the pan from the heat and carefully stir in the vegetables. Season to taste, serve sprinkled with chopped parsley. Serve the cheese separately in case you love it just as it is.

•• If there is any left you can warm it through very gently with a little more water.

CREAMY VANILLA RICE PUDDING

The art of a rice pudding is to cook it very slowly and to avoid skimmed milk which never gives the thick creamy texture desired.

Using a vanilla pod in a rice pudding lifts it from invalid food to gourmet comfort food. Vanilla pods are expensive but they are a good investment and they can be used 5-6 times before delegating them to making a final batch of vanilla sugar. You have to rinse the vanilla pod well in warm water after each use, leave it to dry and then store it in a sealed container full of caster sugar. You can then cook with the vanilla sugar after 4-5 days.

To give a strong flavour to any pudding or for custard simply slit the vanilla pod along its length and with the tip of a sharp knife, scrape out some of the tiny black seeds into your liquid. Add the split pod as well. Remove the pod before serving. Serves 4

15g/ 1/2oz dairy-free sunflower spread
85g/3oz/1/2 cup short grained pudding
   rice and 1 tablespoon ground rice
45g/11/2oz/1/4 cup caster sugar
2 teaspoons pure vanilla extract

1 litre/13/4 pints/4 cups unsweetened
   dairy-free soya milk
Optional: strawberry jam or thick raspberry
   purée to serve

•• Preheat the oven to 150C/300F/Gas 2.

1) Smear the sunflower spread thickly around the base and sides of an ovenproof dish.
2) Scatter the rice and ground rice, sugar, vanilla extract and the soya milk together in the dish and stir briefly.
3) Cook for 1 hour, remove the pudding from the oven, break the skin, so that you can stir the rice and return to the oven to cook for 1/2 hour more. Let the rice cool for about 15 minutes before serving so that it thickens into a creamy pudding.

•• Eat the rice pudding hot or warm with jam. As the pudding cools it will absorb more milk so if you are not eating it within an hour or two, then you may need to stir in more milk to prevent it becoming too solid.

FISH AND SEAFOOD

Fish is so quick and easy to cook that I think of it as a fast/convenience food which unlike some foods I could mention actually is full of goodness and has a wide range of tastes. There are so many different kinds of texture, from the small firm flakes of some white fish to the big meaty solidness of fish like tuna. The biggest concern is the freshness of seafood. It is not something that can be stored at the back of the fridge for a few days but needs to be eaten fresh within 24 hours of purchase. Usually the virtuousness I feel at the low calories and health-giving values of my fish or seafood is enough to counteract the time and energy it takes to find the fishmonger in the market.

There are several ways of procuring fish, the easiest being neatly packed, ready prepared and odour free in the supermarkets but it is so much better to choose your own fresh fish from the food counter. The other option, which I prefer, is to go to a fishmonger. If you suffer from food allergies then it will suddenly become impossible to buy even good quality ready-made dishes from even the best stores or supermarkets as they will inevitably have wheat or dairy or both. Therefore in this section I have chosen familiar recipes which would otherwise be an impossible quest until you come across a company that specializes in fish products by mail order.

The trouble with packaged fish is that your choice is very limited and as the fish is packaged you cannot see or smell the reality of the fish's freshness. It may taste fine but just have that tang of having hung around for a few days.

The other disadvantage of packaged or fish counter seafood is that you cannot discuss the types of fish or ask questions. For example which species could be used to replace the one decidedly absent from the counter for your recipe that evening?

You should also be able to get fish exactly how you want it, for example it might need to be scaled, beheaded, skinned and boned etc., and for this the fishmonger is infinitely better. He will also be able to help you with quantities and unlike the supermarket will know exactly where and when the fish was caught and probably how! This will give you real freshness.

As this is paramount when choosing fish there are one or two important guidelines for you. Stale seafood tastes dull and boring and of course can give you a jippy tummy in the worst cases. First of all use your nose and if the fish smells at all fishy then it is past its prime. If anything then it should have just a whiff of the sea, loch or river it came from. The next clear indication is the clearness of its eyes. They should be bright, raised and glassy. The older the fish is the more the eyes have a milky haze spread over them and they sink down into the head. The next indicator is the colour of the gills; they should be bright and have a clean pinkish hue not dull brown. You need to probe the fish to discover this which is obviously impossible if it is pre-packaged. Lastly, the flesh needs to be firm and pearly and not soft and cotton-woolly; any gaps in the surface flesh are bad news and the fish should be avoided at all costs.

Taking care of your fish is also important. You must get it into the fridge as quickly as possible, don't leave it in the car or at work for hours on end. Always let the fish get back to room temperature about 15-20 minutes before you need it. If you are defrosting fish or seafood then make sure that you do so thoroughly and don't be tempted to speed it up with boiling water or the microwave.

The hidden perils of fish are few so I don't know why we are all so scared of dealing with them – overcooking is the one and only no-no. Under-cooking by the odd minute is fine, safe and often taste and texture enhancing. So do veer towards under-cooking rather than to over-cooking. Bear in mind that fish carries on cooking even when it is out of the pan just through its own heat.

You can easily check if the fish is cooked simply by poking it with a sharp knife in a discreet place. When the flesh is cooked it comes away from the bone with ease but the flesh should still feel firm. If it gets mushy you have blown it!

The best ways to cook fish vary to the species of course but generally thinner fillets of fish, small whole flat fish and trout are great fried in a little olive oil or sunflower spread. Pat the fish dry with kitchen paper and get the pan really hot before cooking. The fish should be hot enough if it sizzles and splutters. Leave the fish alone, I know it is tempting but don't touch it! Allow at least 1 minute for thin fish and 3 for thicker pieces. The fish then browns underneath and unsticks itself from the pan which should prevent the destruction of the fish in one fell swoop as you lift it out and it disintegrates. Speed is essential for the best results but if you have trout then you will need to reduce the heat and cook for a bit longer.

Searing and griddling fish is much the same process only the thick-based pan has ridges which gives you neat brown stripes on your fish rather like a barbecue. This method of cooking only suits whole or very solid fish like salmon, tuna and swordfish.

Poaching fish is absolutely the opposite, it is quiet and gentle and keeps the fish moist. The water or sauce should barely tremble when cooking the fish. The water, stock, milk or wine is simmering when the bubbles start to stream up to the surface of the liquid, at this point remove the dish from the direct heat or you will massacre the fish.

Steaming fish is also a damp and gentle method of cooking and preserves the flavour and texture. This is very easy with the correct equipment but failing that you can simply wrap the fish with some seasoning, lemon juice and water, sunflower spread and herbs in a big pocket of foil. Place the wrapped fish in a dish and cook gently in the oven.

PLAICE FLORENTINE

I logged on to various internet sites to find out which fish are the most endangered and which are relatively abundant and came up with what I hope is a selection of fish recipes which I feel comfortable eating. Plaice are beautiful creatures dotted with bright orange spots. Here is another opportunity to practice your white sauce to perfection. Serves 4

Dairy-free sunflower spread
White sauce, recipe page 41
450g/1lb packet of washed spinach leaves
4 generous fresh plaice fillets or any sustainable thick white fish fillet or steaks, skinned

Parmazano dairy-free grated cheese (see stockists) or either goats' or pecorino cheese
Cayenne pepper

•• Preheat the oven to 180C/350C/Gas 5. Smear some sunflower spread around a gratin dish (oven-to-table baking dish).
•• Don't forget to bring the fish to room temperature 15 minutes before starting the recipe.

1) Make the white sauce and set aside.
2) Cook the spinach leaves in boiling water for a couple of minutes, they should literally just be wilted. Drain and rinse under cold water to preserve their colour and stop them cooking any longer.
3) Cover the base of the dish with the spinach leaves. Take the fish and pat dry with kitchen paper. Fold the fillets in half if you are using flat fish into neat parcels and sit them on the spinach making sure that they are evenly spaced for easy serving. If you are using thick fillets or steaks then just cut into 4 portions.
4) Pour the white sauce over the fish, sprinkle with Parmazano or goats'/pecorino cheese and finish with a very light dusting of cayenne pepper.
5) Bake in the oven for about 20 minutes or until the sauce is lightly golden and bubbling around the edges. Serve immediately.

SALMON FISH CAKES

You can make these fish cakes with any kind of leftover poached, fresh, smoked or canned fish. Even people known not to like fish much tend to enjoy fishcakes so it is a fairly safe cheap family meal. It is a good way of using up stale bread as fresh breadcrumbs really don't work. Makes 8

450g/1lb fresh skinless salmon fillets
2 bay leaves
150ml/1/4 pint/1/2 cup + 2 tablespoons unsweetened dairy-free soya milk
350g/12oz floury potatoes such as Maris Piper
25g/1oz dairy-free sunflower spread
Sea salt and freshly ground black pepper

1 large egg, beaten
Doves Farm gluten-free plain flour
100g/31/2oz/3/4 cup Orgran gluten-free rice crumbs or home-made breadcrumbs
2 tablespoons sunflower oil
Optional: Tomato ketchup and wedges of lemon

1) Lay the fish in a frying pan with the bay leaves and soya milk. Add 150ml/1/4 pint/1/2 cup + 2 tablespoons water to the milk and let the fish poach gently until it is just opaque. Remove from the heat and leave for 10 minutes.

2) Peel and chop the potatoes and put them into a pan of boiling water. Boil until they are soft, drain and leave them for 5 minutes.

3) Return the potatoes to the pan; mash them with the sunflower spread and season with salt and pepper. Gently flake the fish into the potato and mix until it holds together but isn't mushy.

4) Pour the beaten egg onto a plate. Sprinkle a thick layer of flour onto another plate and lastly a thick layer of breadcrumbs on a third plate.

5) Divide the fish mixture into 8 and with floured hands shape them and coat them with the flour on the plate. Then sit each cake in the egg, brush over the top and sides and finally dip and roll the cakes in the breadcrumbs.

6) Transfer them to a clean plate, chill and cover until needed or cook straight away. Heat the oil in a large frying pan over medium heat. The fish cakes should sizzle but if they cook too quickly they will burn on the outside and be cold inside.

7) Cook 4 fish cakes at a time until they turn golden brown. Turn them over and when both sides are crisp and golden they are ready to serve.

COLEY GOUJONS WITH AIOLI

This is my version of fish fingers, easy for children to help make and eat! They might prefer tomato ketchup instead of the suggested aioli. Serve with a mixed salad for grown ups and peas for children. Serves 4

150g/5oz/1 cup of Orgran gluten-free all purpose crumbs

Sea salt and freshly ground black pepper

2 large eggs

Plain gluten-free flour for dusting

Sprinkling of cayenne pepper (adults only)

450g/1lb skinned and boned sustainable white fish fillets (coley)

Sunflower oil for shallow frying

Serve with wedges of lemon and a bowl of aioli (recipe page 20-21)

1) Put the crumbs on a large plate and season them with salt and pepper.
2) Beat the eggs in a shallow bowl with a fork.
3) Sieve some flour onto a large plate and sprinkle with cayenne.
4) Cut the fish into bite size strips with a sharp knife on a chopping board. Dust them first with the sifted flour to help the egg stick onto the fish pieces. Then dip the goujons into the beaten egg followed by a dip and roll in the breadcrumbs, coating evenly.
5) Heat the oil in a large frying pan and fry the goujons for a few minutes on each side until crisp and golden on the outside and cooked and opaque inside. This will of course depend on how thickly you cut the fish and which kind of fish you have used. Test one and then get a feel for the timing for the remaining goujons. If you need a bit more oil then let it heat up before frying the next batch.

SEARED SQUID WITH CHORIZO

This is an easy and quick spicy dish which you can make while sipping a glass of chilled rosé wine. It is delicious with a selection of salads such as roasted peppers and aubergines and a green leaf salad. I use frozen squid but you can use unfrozen if you prefer. Serves 4

500g/1lb 2oz frozen baby squid, defrosted

4 tablespoons olive oil

225g/8oz good quality chorizo (about half the "U" shaped Spanish sausage), thinly sliced

2 large cloves garlic, crushed

400g/14oz can chickpeas in salted water

200g/7oz sun dried tomatoes in oil, drained weight

A sprinkling of hot paprika to your taste

Sea salt and freshly ground black pepper

Fresh lemon juice to taste

2 large handfuls fresh coriander leaves, chopped

1) Rinse the squid under cold running water, pull out the transparent quill if there is one and discard. Keep the tentacles.
2) Dry the squid and tentacles on kitchen paper. Heat half the oil in a huge griddling pan over high heat. Throw in the squid and shake around for a few minutes until seared and opaque.
3) Transfer the squid into a large warm dish. In the same pan over medium heat toss the chorizo, tentacles, garlic, chickpeas, tomatoes and paprika. Cook until the ingredients are hot, season to taste and remove from the heat.
4) Toss the mixture in with the squid, sprinkle with lemon juice and as many coriander leaves as you like and serve immediately.

SPICED MACKEREL WITH RAITA

Oily fish being so good for us I have devised an easy and cheap dish which can be prepared earlier in the day and cooked quickly at the last minute or even barbecued. The raita can be made with any sort of plain yogurt that you can tolerate. Serves 4

1 tablespoon coriander seeds

16 cardamom pods, split and seeds scooped out

5cm/2in piece peeled root ginger, finely chopped

1/2 teaspoon ground cloves

Sea salt and freshly ground black pepper

4 tablespoons olive oil

4 fresh mackerel, gutted (cleaned), beheaded and washed under cold running water

2 tablespoons chopped fresh coriander leaves

Raita

375ml/13fl.oz/1 1/2 cups natural soya or goats' yogurt

1 large garlic clove, crushed

2 heaped tablespoons finely chopped fresh mint leaves

4 heaped tablespoons grated raw baby courgettes

1) In a large frying pan heat the coriander and cardamom seeds for 2-3 minutes.

2) Pound or process the hot spices with the ginger, cloves, salt, pepper and oil in a pestle and mortar until you achieve a coating consistency.

3) Alternatively, use the smaller bowl and blade fitting of the food processor normally reserved for herbs and baby food.

4) Slash the skin of the fish diagonally on both sides and smear both sides with the spice mixture.

5) Sauté the fish in the pan, over medium heat, until both sides are crispy and the flesh is cooked through and opaque.

6) Meanwhile, make the raita by mixing the yogurt, garlic, mint and grated courgettes together in a small bowl. Season to taste with salt and pepper.

7) Transfer the cooked mackerel to a warm serving dish, sprinkle with the coriander and serve immediately, accompanied by the bowl of raita.

FISH PIE

To me this is comfort food of the best kind with creamy mashed potato and piping hot thick sauce underneath but it is certainly good enough for a dinner party too. Add prawns or scallops for a more extravagant version. You can also replace the smoked fish with salmon if you want a change. Serves 6

1kg/2lb 2oz floury potatoes, peeled and cut into chunks

Dairy-free unsweetened soya milk and sunflower spread

Sea salt and freshly ground black pepper

White sauce, recipe page 41

4 large eggs

450g/1lb skinless coley fillets, diced into even sized cubes

450g/1lb skinless smoked haddock fillets, diced into even sized cubes

200g/7oz can sweetcorn kernels, drained

4 tablespoons frozen peas

A large handful of fresh parsley leaves, finely chopped

A dusting of cayenne pepper

•• Preheat the oven to 200C/400F/Gas 6.

1) Boil the potatoes until soft, drain and return them to the pan. Mash them with just enough soya milk and sunflower spread to make a soft mash. If it is too solid it won't spread easily over the fish in sauce but if it is too soft it will just melt into a gloopy mess with the sauce. Season to taste.

2) Meanwhile, make the white sauce according to the recipe.

3) Hard boil the eggs in boiling water for 8 minutes, drain and rinse under cold running water to prevent them overcooking and turning grey around the edges of the yolk. Peel the eggs as soon as they are cool enough, quarter, roughly chop and set them aside.

4) Take a deep pie or gratin dish (oven-to-table) and pour in half the white sauce. Cover the sauce with the cubes of fish making sure that the mixture is even. Scatter over the eggs, sweetcorn, frozen peas and parsley.

5) Cover as lightly as you can with the mashed potato, starting at the edge and working inwards. Push the mash right to the edge to seal. Fluff the top with a fork and dot with tiny bits of sunflower spread and a dusting of cayenne pepper.

6) Bake in the oven for about 30 minutes or until the top is golden, the edges of the sauce bubbling and the fish is cooked through. Serve immediately.

SCALLOP AND PRAWN NOODLES WITH LIME

Thai is stylish, fun and easy but I tend to eat this kind of simplified westernized version which has a few less exotic ingredients without losing its lively tastes or textures. Do not use fine noodles as they are difficult to incorporate with the other ingredients. Serves 3

1/2 medium chilli, deseeded and finely chopped

1 tablespoon Meridian Free From Tamari Soya sauce

1 tablespoon runny honey

1 tablespoon sesame seeds

Finely grated zest and juice of 2 unwaxed limes

Sea salt and freshly ground black pepper

100g/3¹/2oz sugar snap peas

115g/4oz baby corn

100g/3¹/2oz King Soba brown rice flat noodles

4 trimmed spring onions, shredded

115g/4oz frozen peeled cooked prawns, defrosted

115g/4oz frozen scallops, defrosted and halved

2 tablespoons sunflower oil

Large handful of coriander leaves, chopped

1) Mix the chilli, soya sauce, honey, seeds, lime zest and juice, salt and pepper together in a little bowl.

2) Put the sugar snap peas and baby corn in one bowl with a little salt, pour over boiling water and leave for 10 minutes to blanch. Then in another bowl repeat this process for only 5 minutes with the noodles.

3) Meanwhile, sauté the spring onions with the prawns and scallops in the oil for a couple of minutes or until the seafood is opaque.

4) Drain the vegetables and the noodles and transfer both to a large warm serving bowl.

5) Pour the sauce into the pan with the seafood to heat through. Toss into the noodle mixture and sprinkle with coriander. Serve immediately.

POULTRY, GAME AND MEAT

Cooking meat and poultry is not really tricky but it depends on two important things; using high-quality produce and neither over-cooking it nor under-cooking it. Like a bottle of wine, if you start off with a good product it is likely to remain a good product and this is as true for the cheap cuts of meat as it is for the expensive. Expensive meat is used for roasting and frying and cheap and succulent cuts for stews, pies and mince. The deciding factors of quality are the breed, husbandry, feed, butchery, hanging time and storage.

The obvious benefit of shopping from an independent butcher is that they can tell you all this information in the shop as you are choosing and buying. The supermarket buyers are not the ones who serve you and hence you do not have access to this information. The supermarkets have less choice of cuts and breeds but it is packaged and ready-prepared. The thing I really value at the butchers is being able to ask how many the joint will serve or how should I cook a certain cut of meat for the best results. Sometimes it is also good to find out why the meat is a certain colour or if the ham has wheat or water or both in it.

I like to buy meat from the farmers' market as you can find some really unusual breeds with superb taste and often cheaper than in the butcher. Free-range produce always tastes better, it is usually sweeter and with a more lingering flavour. If you buy produce that is intensively reared then you get what you pay for.

The hanging of poultry, game and meat is vital to the quality of the finished product. Hanging in controlled temperatures makes the meat more tender and succulent. The longer meat is hung, for example 21 days, the more the flavour is enhanced and the darker the colour appears. So if you see bright red beef or lamb, beware! Watch out for a grey tinge though because this means that the meat has gone too far and even if it is on special offer don't be tempted as it will not taste any good.

Keep raw produce in the fridge, sitting in a shallow dish, wrapped loosely in greaseproof paper and make sure than it cannot contaminate other products by dripping blood anywhere other than in the dish. If you have had your produce in a hot car or your fridge is too warm then be watchful for it going off before the sell by date. If the produce comes from a butcher it won't have a label with this information so use common sense and watch out for any nasty smell.

There isn't a piece of meat, poultry or game that won't benefit from resting after cooking. This means leaving it alone in a warm place so that the meat re-absorbs its juices and spreads them evenly around the flesh. Amazing really that this is what makes it taste so much juicier. This not only means that less liquid oozes out when you carve but it also gives you time to make the gravy or sauce and finish off the vegetables. Larger joints and whole birds need about 20 minutes rest and huge joints about 30 minutes. Even small steaks and chops should rest for 4 minutes.

Roasting is best suited for whole birds and larger cuts of meat or game. Venison needs a day or two of marinating before roasting but should be fine to casserole. Most people seem perfectly happy to roast a chicken but blanch at the thought of a game bird or Sunday roast. As we have said the buying of the roast is almost the most important factor and it is essential to make sure that it is marbled with fat to ensure it remains full of flavour and moist. So don't be tempted by the leanest meat or you will be disappointed. Pork benefits from a thick layer of fat under the crackling to prevent drying out and to ensure the crackling crackles.

There is nothing extra to do, just remember to baste it every so often and make sure the heat is high enough. Basting means to spoon hot cooking juices back over the meat as it cooks to keep it moist and enhance the flavour. Do this every 30-45 minutes depending on the size and length of cooking time. Pork is the exception and it is not basted, unless you don't want crackling and it should be thoroughly cooked.

The waft of a crispy roast chicken is to me a total joy but do spare a thought for where it has come from. If it has come from a free-range happy environment it will taste as fabulous as it looks. If it has had a sad life, caged up with no exercise and unable to peck at the ground it will taste of very little. Cooped up chickens are cheap but definitely not cheerful.

Even more scrupulous care is needed for the storage and preparation of chicken. Salmonella is undoubtedly to be avoided so keep it away from raw foods and wash all your utensils etc. before doing anything else in the kitchen. Remove the string from the trussed chicken as with legs open wide the air can freely circulate and it will cook more efficiently. This reduces the possibility of raw inner thighs and over-cooked breast. Basting the bird makes for crispier skin and moist flesh. Spoon the juices over the breast area in particular and quickly return to the oven.

It is worth calculating the cooking time correctly as the more haphazard you are the more likely the vegetables etc. will be over or under-cooked. It has been known in our household that our guests have had to wait an extra hour because of my chaotic timing which meant another couple of bloody marys and a rather flustered hostess!

A delicious stew or casserole is so comforting when the weather is cold but it is also marvellous for entertaining as it is best when made the day before. The flavour matures and enhances and the process of reheating helps to make the meat tender and melting, unless you overcooked it in the first place. While not quick to prepare stewing is easy, stress, mess and odour free when entertaining. To stew means to cook the meat with vegetables, aromatics and liquids for a fairly long time. Stews are usually cheap to make because of the inexpensive cuts, especially with chicken when you can use thighs and drumsticks. Usually the recipe will tell you which cut of meat to use because the meat suffuses all the other ingredients in the dish and ensures the complex flavours of the sauce. Do not cut the cubes of meat into very small pieces or they will disintegrate but make sure they are of an even size and any gristle and large chunks of fat are removed.

Just a word of advice on seasoned flour and casseroles whether you are using gluten-free or not – avoid tossing the meat in the flour too early or it will become sticky and gluey. Add salt and pepper to the flour just before cooking for the best results. As for the casserole dish, it needs to be thick and heavy so that the stew is less likely to catch or burn at the bottom and the heat will be more evenly distributed than in a cheaper and thinner-based dish. The lid must fit snugly and the dish needs to be big enough because if the stew is all squashed up then it will not cook properly. I have a china casserole dish which is really annoying because you cannot put it on the hob if it needs finishing off in some way at the end of the cooking time, a cast iron one would be much better and it does last a life time.

As far as cooking the stew, casserole or mince goes it is important to brown the meat in hot fat first. This is called 'sealing' and it gives an appealing colour to the meat, brings extra flavour and helps produce a rich colour for the sauce. If you overcrowd the pan the meat will stew in its own juices so it is much better to cook in 2-3 batches. Leave the meat alone while it browns for about 3 or more minutes and then turn over repeatedly until all the other sides are browned. Transfer the pieces to a warm plate until they are all done.

No recipe is perfect so sometimes you do have to thicken or thin a stew or casserole or even gravy. You can boil the sauce down a bit until it is thicker or add cornflour dissolved in cold water and stirred into the hot liquid. Never add undissolved cornflour to hot liquid or it will congeal and not do the job at all. Heat the sauce until the cornflour has turned the sauce clear again. You can of course make a beurre manié with dairy-free sunflower spread and gluten-free flour – proceed as with a normal recipe but use much smaller amounts at a time to prevent lumps forming.

ROAST PHEASANT WITH GRAVY AND BREAD SAUCE

I have the advantage of living in the heart of Shropshire countryside and pheasants are literally running in front of you on your autumn and winter walks. I have tried so many different recipes but at the end of the day I don't think you can beat traditional roast pheasant with all the trimmings. Serves 6

Bread Sauce, see recipe page 45

Roast Pheasant

1 small onion and carrot, peeled and chopped

2 bay leaves

Few sprigs thyme or rosemary

1 large clove garlic, chopped

1 small wine glass white wine or cider and the same again of stock

2 large ready-to-cook pheasants

At least 6 slices of streaky bacon

Olive oil

Sea salt and freshly ground black pepper

Gravy

See recipe page 44

Optional extras: gluten-free chipolata or cocktail sausages and roast potatoes

•• Preheat the oven to 190C/375F/Gas 5.

1) Make the bread sauce first as it needs to infuse. Then start on the roast potatoes if you are doing them followed by the roast pheasant. If you want to have sausages then they must be cooked in another roasting tin about half-way through the pheasant cooking time.

2) Place the vegetables, herbs, garlic and liquid around a roasting tin. Wrap each pheasant with bacon rashers to cover the breast and meaty bit of the leg to help prevent the birds from drying out.

3) Place the pheasants on top of the vegetables and brush with oil and season with pepper. You can sprinkle a little salt around the birds but if you put salt on the bacon it will be rather over powering.

4) Roast for 1 hour and then remove from the oven. Check the birds are cooked and that there are no pink juices running out of the legs. It is best to do this with a skewer or very sharp knife. Carefully lift the birds out and onto a carving board and cover loosely with foil to keep warm.

5) Leave the pheasants to sit while you make the gravy, finish off the bread sauce and take care of all the other extras. Keep everything warm until you are ready to carve and serve.

6) Carve the pheasants as you would a chicken, that is thinly sliced breast and legs for anyone who wants one with the breast. Serve with all the other goodies.

GRIDDLED CHICKEN AND PESTO SALAD

This salad is delicious warm or cold and is best served with baby new potatoes and a tomato, avocado and basil salad. Also the chargrilled courgette and mint salad (recipe page 36) works well. Serves 4

3 large or 4 small chicken breasts sliced
   into strips
Olive oil to brush chicken and cook
   croûtons
Rocket pesto, (1/2 quantity of recipe page
   46)

Sea salt and freshly ground black pepper
1 large cos lettuce, trimmed and sliced
2 thick slices gluten-free white bread, crusts
   removed (see stockists)

1) Brush the chicken pieces with plenty of oil. Cook the pieces until opaque and tender in a large chargrill pan.
2) Meanwhile, prepare the pesto sauce. Put the salad in a serving dish.
3) Make the croûtons: cut the bread into small cubes, fry them in a little oil until golden all over. You can use the same pan.
4) Arrange the chicken pieces over the salad and spoon blobs of pesto all over. Sprinkle with the croûtons and serve warm.

•• For a chilled salad it is best to prepare everything in advance and put the dish together at the last minute to prevent a soggy lettuce situation!

WARM ROAST DUCK AND FIG SALAD

Fresh figs are often available out of season but I prefer to save air miles and eat this delicious salad when figs are plentiful in the market. Don't buy them with bruised or spoiled skin. Figs hate the cold so don't refrigerate them. I buy free-range duck breasts but for a cheaper salad you could use the legs and cook them for longer. Serves 2

2 duck breasts, skin on
1 tablespoon balsamic vinegar
2 tablespoons clear honey
1 heaped teaspoon fresh thyme leaves
1 large clove garlic, finely chopped

Zest and juice 1 unwaxed orange
Sea salt and freshly ground black pepper
4 large fresh and ripe figs, halved
2 large handfuls of mixed salad leaves

1) Heat a large frying pan over medium heat and cook the duck breasts gently, skin side down for about 15–20 minutes depending on the size. The duck should be pink inside and crispy skinned on the outside.
2) Drain off the fat and discard. Transfer the duck to a warm plate.
3) Put the balsamic vinegar, honey, thyme, garlic, zest and juice of the orange and seasoning into the pan and cook for 5 minutes. Add the fig halves to the pan and cook for a few minutes until sticky and slightly softened.
4) Place a large handful of salad on each plate and carve the duck breasts into neat slices. Place the slices on the salad. Arrange the figs around the salad, drizzle with the juices and serve.

CHICKEN TIKKA PITTA BREADS

I love pitta bread but it was years until some really good gluten-free pitta appeared on the market. They should be made with gram flour but some manufacturers put wheat in to make them cheap. There are some really good bottled curry sauces around. Cooked prawns are also delicious in this recipe. Makes 1

1 heaped tablespoon Meridian Tikka Masala or Korma sauce or Mr Patak's Jalfrezi sauce

2 heaped tablespoons chopped cooked chicken breast

1 tablespoon home-made mayonnaise (recipe page 20)

Sea salt and freshly ground black pepper

1 gluten-free pitta bread (Tesco Free From are the best)

1 small vine ripened tomato, skinned and thinly sliced

2-3 heaped tablespoons finely sliced fennel

Optional: Fresh coriander leaves

1) In a small frying pan heat the chosen curry sauce and stir in the chicken. Reheat the chicken until just warm or you will melt the mayonnaise!

2) Transfer the mixture to a bowl, cool for 5 minutes, mix in the mayonnaise and season to taste.

3) Heat the pitta bread in the toaster and once it is puffy and hot then quickly slice half the way through it at the seam. You can now make a pocket which can be filled.

4) Spoon in the chicken with the tomatoes and fennel. Serve immediately scattered with some torn coriander leaves.

CAJUN TURKEY BURGERS

This is a low fat version of a burger and is delicious with gluten-free pickles, your own salsa or tomato ketchup with a dash of chilli in it. You can also use pork in this recipe. Lots of lovely salads make this a fun and healthy meal. Makes 4

Burger
500g/1lb 2oz free-range turkey mince
85g/3oz/1¾ cups fresh gluten-free white breadcrumbs, (stockist page 166)
1 teaspoon Cajun spice powder
Pinch of sea salt and freshly ground black pepper
4 spring onions, trimmed and finely chopped
1 large egg, beaten
1 tablespoon sunflower oil

Mango Salsa
½ large ripe mango, peeled, sliced and very finely chopped
A large handful coriander leaves, finely chopped
Zest and juice 1 unwaxed lime
1 medium red or green chilli, deseeded and finely chopped
2 tablespoons cooked sweetcorn kernels, (canned or frozen)
Optional: 4 x pack gluten-free white burger buns (see stockists)
Serve with Geeta's premium mango chutney or any gluten-free chutney

1) Put the mince, breadcrumbs, spice, seasoning, spring onions and egg together in a big bowl. Mix well with your hands.
2) Divide into 4 and shape into burgers. Chill for 20 minutes or more.
3) Meanwhile make the salsa. Mix all the ingredients together in a serving bowl and set aside.
4) Brush the burgers with oil and cook under a hot grill for 10 minutes on each side or until the meat is completely cooked through. Alternatively cook on the barbecue. Serve each burger in a bun with the salsa and chutney.

VENISON SAUSAGES WITH RED CABBAGE

The important tip for this recipe is to cook the sausages until they are really well browned as they will not brown when cooking with the cabbage. Your butcher, if he deals in venison, will make you up a large quantity of venison gluten-free sausages for freezing. You need big and chunky ones and should allow about 3 per person. You can also find mail order venison sausages on the internet. Red cabbage brings much needed colour in winter and can be frozen too. Serves 4-5

1 tablespoon olive oil
1 very large onion, halved and finely sliced
12 large thick venison sausages (for Sally's Sizzlers see page 167)
2 tablespoons demerara sugar
2 bay leaves
1 heaped teaspoon ground cloves
2 heaped teaspoons ground allspice
800g/1³/4lb red cabbage, tough outer layers removed, quartered and trimmed of core, very finely sliced (no more than 600g/1¹/4lb)

2 heaped tablespoons raisins
Sea salt and freshly ground black pepper
125ml/4fl.oz/¹/2 cup balsamic and cider vinegar mixed in equal parts
125ml/4fl.oz/¹/2 cup leftover port or hearty red wine
30g/1oz sunflower dairy-free spread

1) Heat the oil in a thick-based casserole dish, add the onions and cook gently until softened. Remove them from the pan onto a plate and then add the sausages and cook over higher heat until they are all evenly browned.
2) Stir the onions back into the casserole of sausages and sprinkle with the sugar. Cook for about 5 minutes until sticky and caramelized.
3) Reduce the heat to medium, throw in the bay leaves, spices, cabbage, raisins and seasoning and stir until combined. Sprinkle over the vinegar mix and the port or wine and cook for about 40 minutes with the lid on. Stir occasionally but be careful not to break up the sausages.
4) Remove the casserole lid and stir the mixture again. Cook the casserole until all the liquid evaporates and the cabbage is sticky, glossy and soft and the sausages are tender and browned.
5) Adjust the seasoning if necessary and mix in the sunflower spread.

•• Serve with mashed or baked potatoes. For a party gratin dauphinoise (page 34) is perfect.

STEAK, KIDNEY AND MUSHROOM PIE

This recipe is very adaptable. You can change it to using only the mushrooms or only kidneys, if you don't eat one or the other. This traditional British dish is made with ale, fortunately now you can buy gluten-free beer or lager from health food shops and stores so we can all enjoy it. Serves 6

1x 500g/1lb 2oz Lovemore Free From gluten-free frozen puff pastry (see stockists)
750g/1lb 10oz diced stewing steak
450g/1lb ox kidney, diced (ask your butcher to prepare it)
255g/9oz mushrooms, wiped clean, peeled if necessary and sliced
55g/2oz/heaped 1/3 cup pure cornflour
Sea salt and freshly ground black pepper
1 teaspoon mustard powder

1 onion, halved and very thinly sliced
1 tablespoon olive oil
1 tablespoon tomato purée
1 teaspoon of chopped thyme
330ml/12fl.oz/1 1/3 cups gluten-free ale
1 tablespoon Life Free From gluten-free Worcestershire sauce
1 bay leaf
1 beaten egg for brushing
Rice flour for dusting and rolling

•• Preheat the oven to 170C/325F/Gas 3.
•• You will need a 2 litre/3 1/2 pint capacity pie dish.

1) Defrost the frozen puff pastry and then keep it chilled until needed.

2) Mix the steak, kidney and mushrooms with the cornflour, salt and pepper and toss until well covered. Put the mixture into the dish and sprinkle with mustard powder. In a large frying pan cook the onions until softened in hot olive oil.

3) Stir the onions, tomato purée and thyme into the meat. Pour over the ale and the Worcestershire sauce and lastly add the bay leaf.

4) Give everything a final mix and then cover the dish with foil or a lid and cook for about 1 1/2 hours or until the meat is tender. The mixture should look thick and glossy.

5) Once the meat is cooked remove the dish from the oven and cool for 20 minutes whilst you bring the pastry to room temperature.

6) At the same time increase the oven heat to 200C/400F/Gas 6.

7) Wet the rim of the dish with cold water or brush with beaten egg. Use a floured rolling pin to roll out the pastry on a floured surface to the required size with a slight overhang. Cut strips off the edge of the pastry to fit the rim of the dish. Stick the strips flat all around the rim of the dish. Wet this pastry either with water or egg and lift the remaining pastry over the pie dish.

8) Seal using your fingers and slice any pastry remnants off with a sharp knife. Brush the pastry with beaten egg and bake for about 25 minutes or until golden and puffy. Serve immediately.

SAUSAGE ROLLS

After 15 years of not eating sausage rolls I am thrilled to have found a puff pastry that works. Make them half the size and they are ideal for picnics, drinks parties, children's parties and packed lunches. You can add 1 medium onion, peeled and grated, 1 teaspoon chopped dried sage and a pinch of salt and freshly ground black pepper to make one giant sausage roll. The meat must be cooked through and the pastry golden and puffy. Serve in slices with salads. Makes 20

1x 500g/1lb 2oz quantity Lovemore Free
    From gluten-free, puff pastry
    (see stockists)
Rice flour to dust and roll
1 egg, beaten with 1 tablespoon
    unsweetened dairy-free soya milk
    or water

Filling
450g/1lb gluten-free sausage meat
    (or Sally's Sizzlers with skins removed –
    see page 167)

•• Preheat the oven to 200C/400F/Gas 6.

1) Defrost the pastry and keep chilled until needed.
2) Flour a board or a clean flat surface. Dust the rolling pin with flour and roll out the pastry into a large rectangle. Cut it into three lengths 35.5cm/14in long. Roll each pastry strip, so that it is a bit wider, dusting with more flour.
3) Divide the sausage mixture into three and make three long thin rolls, the same length as the pastry.
4) Place one roll of sausage meat on one roll of pastry. Brush the beaten egg mixture along one edge, then fold the pastry over and seal it as carefully as you can by pressing it down gently with your fingertips.
5) Cut each roll into 5cm/2in long strips. Place the rolls on a baking sheet with the seam-side down.
6) Lightly snip two V shapes with a pair of scissors on top of each roll and brush each one with beaten egg.
7) Bake in the oven for about 20 minutes. The sausage rolls should be cooked inside and the pastry golden and puffy. Serve immediately or store the cooled rolls in a tin and reheat for serving.

VENISON CASSEROLE WITH DUMPLINGS

Looking around the supermarkets this year I was amazed to see that they all had some sort of beef stew with dumplings. So I set about trying to work out a dependable dumpling recipe to go with a traditional beef dish. You can make your favourite beef dish and simply add the dumplings. Serves 6

3 tablespoons olive oil

1kg/2lbs 2oz venison stewing steak, cut into cubes

2 tablespoons Doves Farm gluten-free plain flour with sea salt and freshly ground black pepper

2 large onions, halved and sliced

115g/4oz lardons or rindless streaky bacon bits

2 large cloves garlic, finely chopped

25g/1oz packet dried porcini mushrooms

2 bay leaves

Half a 75cl bottle of hearty red wine

2 large sprigs fresh thyme

1 heaped tablespoon tomato paste

250ml/9fl.oz/1 cup beef or vegetable stock or beef consommé

1x 280-350g/10-12oz jar/packet of sun dried tomatoes in oil, drained weight 140g/5oz

Dumplings

2 teaspoons olive oil

225g/8oz/2 cups Doves Farm gluten-free plain flour

4 level teaspoons gluten-free baking powder

1 heaped teaspoon mustard powder

Pinch of salt and freshly ground black pepper

115g/4oz/1 cup Community Foods gluten-free vegetable suet

1 teaspoon chopped dried sage leaves or double if fresh

Cold water

•• You will need a really big casserole dish.

•• Preheat the oven to 180C/350F/Gas 4.

1) Put 2 tablespoons of oil in the casserole dish over medium heat. Toss the meat in a plate of seasoned flour and cook the steak in one or two batches until all of it is browned. Transfer the browned meat to a warm dish.
2) Reserve 1/4 of the sliced onions for the dumplings.
3) Add the remaining oil, cook the onions and lardons or bacon for a few minutes in the dish until golden and then add the garlic and mushrooms.
4) Put all the meat and juices into the casserole of onions and stir in to mix them all up. Add the bay leaves, wine, thyme and tomato paste and cook for a few minutes.
5) Stir in the stock or consommé and the drained tomatoes and cover the casserole with a lid.
6) Cook the casserole in the oven for about 1 1/2 hours or until the meat is tender, which will depend on the meat you have used. If it needs a lot more time then add more wine or stock to ensure that the sauce remains glossy, thick and rich and doesn't dry out.
7) **Make the dumplings:** finely chop the remaining sliced onions and fry them in the oil until browned and caramelized. Allow them to cool.
8) In a mixing bowl sift the flour, baking powder, mustard powder and a pinch of salt together. Add the suet, sage and the cooked onions and season with some black pepper.
9) Sprinkle a little cold water at a time over these ingredients and using first a knife and then your hands, bring it all together to form a soft dough. The dough just needs to hold together, veering on the dry side. If the dumplings are soggy at the start there is no hope for them.
10) Using clean hands mould about 12 handfuls into balls as big as a whole walnut shell.
11) Add them to the surface of your casserole and gently press them down a little bit. Return the casserole without the lid to the oven and cook for about 30 minutes or until the dumplings are golden brown and crusty. This will depend on how hot the casserole is to start with so timing may vary a lot.

PORK VALDOSTANA

This is a recipe from the north of Italy and is delicious because the sauce isn't too rich, the meat isn't fatty and the bone is nicely trimmed. I serve this dish with crispy fried potato cubes tossed with garlic and rosemary. Serves 4

4 x 225g/8oz loin pork chops
4 x large but thin slices prosciutto
4 large fresh sage leaves
4 slices Tofutti Creamy Smooth mozzarella-style slices or plenty of buffalo mozzarella

2 heaped tablespoons gluten-free plain flour or rice flour
Sea salt and freshly ground black pepper
2 tablespoons olive oil
30g/1oz dairy-free sunflower spread
4 tablespoons Marsala

•• Preheat the oven to 220C/425F/Gas 7.

1) Ask your butcher to French trim the chops or you need to cut around the lower part of the bone, scraping off the fat and as much of the meat as possible. Trim off the fat that surrounds the lean loin part of the chop.
2) Flatten the meat gently with a meat mallet or the end of a rolling pin. Put a slice of prosciutto on a clean surface; place a sage leaf on top, then a slice of cheese, followed by the meaty part of the chop.
3) Wrap the prosciutto around the chop so the meaty part is completely covered.
4) Put the flour on a large plate and season. Hold onto the bone to lay each chop in the flour to coat them on all sides. Heat the oil and sunflower spread in a large ovenproof pan and cook the chops cheese side down for 1 minute.
5) Turn the chops over and cook for a couple of minutes until browned. Pour over the Marsala and bring to the boil. Transfer to the oven and bake for 15-20 minutes until the pork is cooked and tender. Serve immediately with the juices over the top.

CHEATING TACOS

This is a healthy recipe for teenage cooks as they can choose what they want to put inside the tacos. They are ideal for a lunch box or picnic as well as sleep-over suppers. Makes 6

360g/12oz rump beef steak (or 250g/9oz cooked prawns), or use up leftovers like cooked chopped chicken or tuna fish

2 small orange peppers, halved, pith and seeds removed

3 tomatoes, peeled (slash the skins, immerse in boiling water in a bowl until easy to peel)

225g/8oz tub Tofutti Sour Supreme, sour cream alternative

A few teaspoons of lemon juice

Sunflower oil

6 taco shells (pure maize, 15cm/6in) depending on appetites

6 small handfuls washed, shredded lettuce leaves

165g/5¹/2oz can sweetcorn kernels, drained

Sea salt and freshly ground black pepper

1) Use a sharp knife to remove fat and then slice steaks into bite size strips.
2) Clean the knife and finely chop the peppers.
3) Quarter the tomatoes, remove pith and seeds and dice them.
4) Empty the sour cream alternative into a small bowl, use a wooden spoon to stir in a little lemon juice at a time until the mixture is soft and smooth.
5) Heat the taco shells in the oven for a few minutes according to the instructions on the packet.
6) Fry the steak in the same pan until done to your liking. If you are using cooked chicken pieces, cooked prawns or tuna fish then simply have them ready in a dish.
7) To assemble the tacos, fill the shells with a little salad, tomato and pepper. Add the chopped meat, chicken, prawns or tuna fish. Sprinkle with sweetcorn and then cover with a dollop of sour cream mix. Season to taste.

BROAD BEAN, SPINACH AND BACON QUICHE

This is a pretty, green flecked quiche which is easy to make and ideal for picnics and lunch all year round. Serves 6

Shortcrust pastry (see page 119)
6 large eggs
125ml/4¹/2fl.oz/¹/2 cup dairy-free soya
   single cream
Sea salt and freshly ground black pepper
A little freshly grated nutmeg
100g/3¹/2oz baby broad beans

100g/3¹/2oz smoked back bacon, rinds
   removed
100g/3¹/2oz frozen chopped spinach,
   defrosted
4-6 slices Tofutti Creamy Smooth cheddar-
   style dairy-free slices or either goats'
   or pecorino cheese

•• You will need a 24cm/9¹/2in loose-bottomed, deep-fluted tart tin lined with a circle of non-stick paper.
•• Preheat the oven to 180C/350F/Gas 4.

1) First make the pastry, chill and then line the tin according to the recipe on page 119.
2) Meanwhile, use a fork to beat the eggs in a mixing bowl with the cream, seasoning and nutmeg.
3) Cook the broad beans in boiling water for 4 minutes, drain in a colander, cool and then remove skins and discard. Add the beans to the eggs.
4) Grill the bacon until just crispy on both sides. Cool and snip with scissors into small pieces. Mix into the eggs with the fork.
5) Pat the defrosted spinach with a few layers of kitchen paper, pressing firmly to absorb any excess water. Mix the spinach into the eggs.
6) Bake the pastry in the centre of the oven for 25 minutes or until golden and the base is cooked through. Remove from the oven and quickly fill the pastry with the quiche filling using the fork to spread the ingredients evenly.
7) Top with 4-6 slices of cheese, bake in the oven for another 25 minutes or until the quiche is puffy and golden and set. Leave to cool for at least 20 minutes before serving.

BREAD, SCONES AND MUFFINS

Our daily bread is an important part of our diet and the biggest problem of being on a restricted diet is the lack of fibre and nutrients that you find in the long-life or mass market dietary breads for sale. They generally have the disadvantage of tasting dull, dry and well, to be honest nothing remotely like bread! Very few of the products can be successfully made into edible sandwiches and so there is a real need to make bread at home that is not only delicious but healthy too. Even if the bread only makes good sandwiches on the day of baking it is worth the effort.

Traditionally you need just five ingredients to make a loaf of bread: fresh or dried yeast, salt, liquid, sugar and fat. There are six stages of traditional bread making: mixing, kneading, rising, knocking down and proving, baking and cooling. However as we are only dealing with gluten-free breads here there have to be some changes.

In the bread making you still need to mix the dough because all the ingredients need to be incorporated and not lumpy but you don't need to knead the dough because there is no gluten. Some of the dough is made to a batter consistency so you can only pour it into the loaf tins anyway. The proving stage varies tremendously, sourdough can double in size but for traditional yeast dough this is seldom the case and of course soda bread has no proving time and is simply baked on the spot.

Alternative rising agents can be used, such as sourdough or baking powder, not only for variation of taste and texture but also because many people nowadays are following yeast-free diets. These alternative breads all retain the need for salt, liquid and fat; this could call for any combination of ingredients such as water and oil, egg and milk powder or honey and treacle. Herbs, seasoning and spices can be used to make the bread more exotic or contemporary but they also serve to improve the taste when using some of the gluten-free flours.

Once the bread is made and cooled then you can store it for a short time. A bread tin is fine but must have some air circulating in it to prevent mould developing. Alternatively, I think it is best to freeze the bread in slices wrapped up in cling film.

Flour needs to be stored in a cool and dry place so avoid keeping it in a cupboard right over the oven or kitchen sink. If you don't have room for an enamelled storage bin then store each type of flour in different airtight containers. As it is best not to store the flour for a long time, don't buy vast amounts if you don't intend to make lots of bread and pastry over the coming weeks.

The ingredients in these recipes are pure and simple because I feel that if you are somebody with food sensitivity you don't really want to eat a slice of additives and yet you don't want something which will go stale quickly, especially if you are the only one eating the bread. I think that there should be some degree of healthy fibre involved as well as good flavour, moist texture and lightness, a fairly tall order it seems but I am glad to say I now have 2 breads to share with you in this book as well as the other recipes in my previous cookbooks.

I have always felt that a huge effort has to be made in order to end up with palatable or even delicious bread – the mere thought of all the kneading and pounding is enough to put me off and so it was with much eagerness that I set off to the Village Bakery bread making course in Cumbria to see how sourdough, wheat and gluten-free breads are made. The good thing about sourdough is that once the starter is made you can store it in the refrigerator for literally years. So after one slightly time-consuming process you can have years of delicious breads – definitely encouraging!

Here is a brief explanation of the gluten-free flours available in case you want to mix and match with my own suggestions in this book.

Chestnut flour: This is milled from dried and roasted sweet chestnuts and is a useful source of flavour because it is naturally sweet. If too much is used it is overwhelming and expensive. I use no more than 10% of flour weight for breads and pastry and this provides excellent fibre.

Gram (chickpea) flour: milled from the chickpea, it is a good source of fibre, protein and minerals such as iron. Once again this is very nutritious flour and the high protein content gives it a firming and binding effect which is good in pastry and breads. Use a maximum of 10% of flour weight because of the strong bean taste.

Tapioca flour: made by heating the tuberous root of the plant this is then dried into granules for tapioca flakes and flour. This is low in nutrients and merely a useful source of starch. It makes a good bland base and a light texture. Use 10% in breads and 20% in pastry. Too much imparts dustiness.

Buckwheat flour: milled from the de-husked seeds of the buckwheat plant which is an annual belonging to the rhubarb family. The seeds are then crushed into a meal which has a greyish/brown colour and becomes the wholemeal flour we know from blinis and soba noodles. Nutritionally this is excellent, containing rutin which helps prevent heart disease, B vitamins, the amino acid lysine and minerals such as calcium. Use no more than 10% of flour weight in your recipes.

Rice flour: milled from de-husked seeds of Oryza sativa. It is the staple diet of half the world's population. Brown rice flour is more nutritional with more fibre and contains vitamin B1, niacin and minerals. If too much is used it produces a slightly gritty texture. It has little binding power but it is cheap and easy to find and makes a good mixture for baking.

I have used prepared flour mixes that are readily available in supermarkets in this book to make the recipes easier and quicker.

Raising agents

The raising agents that are generally used for gluten free breads are yeast, baking powder and sourdough starter. My two recipes are the yeasted breads which are what most of us are used to and which are more traditional in style and taste. Fresh yeast tends to worry people more because they wonder if it is indeed alive and active or stale and inactive. The dried brands are of course more reliable but check they are gluten free. Here are a few guidelines to help with using yeast.

Fresh yeast should be firm, moist, cream-coloured and cool to touch. Anything that looks dry and crumbly with dark patches is stale and probably inactive. You simply place the yeast in the liquid, dissolve it and mix it into the dough straight away. You can freeze the yeast in 25g/1oz quantities for three months or keep in the refrigerator for up to three days. Fresh yeast needs warmth and some liquid to activate it and then it releases the gas that will raise the dough. This activity stops when the dough is placed in the oven and the extreme temperature kills off the yeast.

Dried yeast on the other hand is reconstituted with warm water and sugar and becomes frothy when active. If it doesn't do this it isn't active and should be discarded. Dried yeast has a time limit too so keep it in an airtight container and stick to the date that is stamped on the packet.

Lastly easy-blend yeast is the quickest of all, nothing to wait for, just sprinkle it into the flour and add the liquid separately.

Two teaspoons of dried yeast is the correct amount for each 450g/1lb flour but easy-blend yeast becomes stale too so watch the date stamp.

The weight equivalents are as follows: 10g fresh yeast

5g active dried yeast

3g fast acting yeast

Pure vitamin C is a helpful raising agent in rye and oat flour yeasted breads.

If you are using salt in the recipes then beware of adding too much as the salt effectively slows down the rising process and too much can actually kill it. If you do add extra salt then allow extra raising time. Sugar is added to the dough mixture to activate dried but not fresh or easy-blend yeast. Molasses or honey can be used for the same purpose but you will end up with a moister loaf.

When you add fats to a dough mixture in larger than normal quantities to make rich fruit buns or loaves this also retards the growth of the yeast, so extra yeast is used. All these breads can be used to make puddings such as bread and butter pudding or apple charlotte or for savoury recipes such as breadcrumbs, croûtes or croûtons.

BREAD WITH CARAWAY AND ALMONDS

This recipe has been adapted from a traditional Greek recipe called Tsoureki and is the Greek equivalent of hot cross buns. The bread is deliciously sweet and so a good contrast to the other bread recipe. Makes 1 large loaf

125ml/1/4 pint/1/2 cup unsweetened
   dairy-free soya milk
125ml/1/4 pint/1/2 cup water
85g/3oz/1/2 cup caster sugar
115g/4oz dairy-free sunflower spread
500g/1lb 2oz/4 heaped cups Doves Farm
   gluten-free white bread flour mix

7g/1/4oz sachet Hovis fast action
   bread yeast
1/4 teaspoon sea salt
1 teaspoon caraway seeds, lightly crushed
3 large eggs
A little oil
2 tablespoons flaked almonds

•• Preheat the oven to 190C/375F/Gas 5. Lightly oil a standard loaf tin.

1) Warm the milk and water in a pan until small bubbles form at the edge.
2) Remove pan from the heat, stir in the sugar and sunflower spread and cool until lukewarm.
3) Mix the flour, yeast, salt and caraway in a large bowl.
4) Beat two eggs in a small bowl.
5) Make a well in the dry ingredients; add the eggs and the milk mixture, then mix. It needs to be a soft sloppy dough.
6) Place in a large bowl and cover with oiled cling film and leave to rise in a very warm place for 2 hours.
7) Gently transfer the dough to an oiled loaf tin and leave until well risen. The dough should leave a dent when gently pressed in the middle.
8) Beat the remaining egg and lightly brush the top of the bread, sprinkle with almonds and bake for about 30 minutes until golden brown and firm to the touch.
9) Leave the bread to cool in the tin and then turn it out onto a wire rack and leave until cold before slicing and serving.

WHITE SEED BREAD

This is the recipe that we now use the most at home because it is so easy, thanks to Glebe Farm. It is baked in a bread machine and it ends up as a large, moist and soft loaf which is perfect for bread on the day of baking or toast thereafter. Makes 1 large loaf

350ml/13fl.oz/1¾ cups unsweetened
   dairy-free soya milk
500g/1lb1oz/4 heaped cups of Glebe Farm
   gluten-free white bread mix
2 large eggs, at room temperature
2 heaped tablespoons mixed seeds (sesame,
   linseed, sunflower and pumpkin)

Optional: 2 heaped teaspoons fresh or dried
   thyme leaves for savoury bread (for
   soups etc.)
The dried yeast packet included in the mix
   or 1 teaspoon of dried yeast

1) Take the bread maker pan out of the machine. Warm the milk to blood temperature in a small pan over low heat.

2) Pour the milk into the bread maker pan; add the flour, then the eggs, seeds, thyme and lastly the yeast. Replace the pan back in the bread-making machine.

3) Select the standard/basic bake programme appropriate to the machine, choosing the extra large loaf and dark crust option.

4) After about 10 minutes, lift the lid of the machine and scrape around the tin with a plastic knife removing flour from the side of the pan and mixing in. Be careful to avoid the paddle if it is moving. Close the lid and leave until finished.

5) Once the baking is completed, carefully lift out the hot pan, leave the bread in the pan for about half an hour and then turn the bread out onto a wire rack to cool.

6) Do not slice until completely cold. Wrap any leftover bread in cling film or an airtight container.

SCONES

Quintessentially English, scones have been transformed from the simple and economical fare of long ago to hybrid modern varieties such as sun dried tomato and goat's cheese or pumpkin and spice. These all appear in magazines and weekend newspaper recipes which is fun and can be made to serve with soups and casseroles over the weekend.

I am going to stick to old fashioned scones because they can be made in minutes by anybody, even children. My daughter is five years old and loves to make them. We can never wait until they have cooled and eat them warm and with home-made jam and local cream.

The great thing about scones is that all the ingredients will be in the cupboard all the time and so they can be made at a drop of a hat. Some recipes do use buttermilk but this is available in all the big supermarkets and is fine for those who can tolerate dairy.

Long ago girdle cakes were made on top of the kitchen range but with the advent of raising agents in flour it was then possible to bake scones in the oven and for them to be well risen.

As far as I can see there are only two potential problems when making scones and these are easily solved.

1) Scones that are too thin and therefore too hard and crusty – the easy remedy is not to roll the dough out too thinly. It should never be less than 2cm/^{3}/$_4$in high. It is always better to make 8 instead of 12 scones but have them light and high and golden.

2) Scones that are wonky – again this is easy, simply roll the scones out very gently and evenly and not pressing down on the rolling pin at one end or the other. When using the cutter don't twist it just stamp it firmly and with floury fingers tease the dough out onto the baking tray.

3) Scones that are doughy and heavy in the middle – just remember to preheat the oven to the high temperature indicated and they should be perfect.

This is the simplest and quickest recipe from all my experimenting with scones over the years. My daughter and I make them all the time as nothing can go wrong with them but they must be made with this flour mix which can be ordered on the internet, see page 166-7 for listing.   Makes 6

115g/4oz/^{3}/$_4$ cup Orgran gluten-free self raising flour
115g/4oz/^{3}/$_4$ cup Doves Farm gluten-free plain flour and a little extra for dusting and shaping
55g/2oz dairy-free sunflower spread

1 tablespoon caster sugar plus a little extra
^{1}/$_2$ teaspoon sea salt
2 teaspoons gluten-free baking powder
1 large egg, beaten and combined with 5 tablespoons unsweetened dairy-free soya milk and a little extra to glaze

•• Preheat the oven 220C/425F/Gas 7.

1) Sift both the flours into a bowl, briefly and lightly rub the sunflower spread in using your fingertips until it resembles breadcrumbs. Stir in the sugar, salt and baking powder.

2) Make a well in the centre of the dry ingredients and stir in the beaten egg and soya milk. Use a blunt ended knife to mix. Flour your clean hands and bring the dough together into a ball, patting it gently. If it is too dry use a few more drops of milk.

3) Turn the dough onto a floured surface and pat it out evenly and gently with the palm of your hand, no less than 2cm/3/4in thick.

4) Use a 5cm/2in floured pastry cutter and place it at the edge of the dough and tap firmly so that it goes straight through the dough without twisting.

5) Cut out 5 dough rounds as close to each other as possible and then use the trimmings to make one more.

6) Place the scones on a floured baking sheet. Brush each one with a little extra soya milk and sprinkle them with a little extra caster sugar.

7) Bake near the top of the oven for about 10-15 minutes. They should be golden brown at the edges, firm and well risen.

•• Cool on a wire rack and eat warm. They are best eaten the same day.

RASPBERRY AND CHOCOLATE MUFFINS

You can use white or milk chocolate if there is no need for dairy free but check that they are gluten free. As with most muffins they are best eaten on the day of baking. Makes 12

285g/10oz/2 + 1/3 cups Doves Farm gluten-free self raising flour, sifted

155g/5oz/3/4 cup unrefined golden caster sugar

2 large eggs

2 teaspoons pure vanilla extract

225ml/8fl.oz/3/4 cup unsweetened dairy-free soya milk

55g/2oz dairy-free sunflower spread, melted

125g/41/2oz/1 cup ripe fresh raspberries

100g/31/2oz Kinnerton Luxury Dark Chocolate, chopped

•• You will need 1 deep muffin tin, lined with 12 large non-stick muffin paper cases.
•• Preheat the oven to 200C/400F/Gas 6.

1) Mix the flour and the sugar in a bowl.

2) Briefly whisk the eggs, vanilla, soya milk and melted sunflower spread in a separate bowl.

3) Stir the liquid mixture into the dry ingredients then briefly and gently fold in the raspberries and chocolate.

4) Spoon the mixture into the prepared muffin tin and bake for about 15-20 minutes until well risen, golden and only just firm to touch as they will carry on cooking for a minute or two in the tin.

5) Serve the muffins warm so that the chocolate is still gooey.

MINI ROSEMARY AND ORANGE MUFFINS

You can easily change the flavouring ingredients to other herbs such as thyme, chopped sage or lavender all of which would go well with lemon. I tried lime and it doesn't really work. Makes 24 mini muffins

55g/2oz dairy-free sunflower spread

85g/3oz/scant 1/2 cup unrefined golden caster sugar

1 large egg, beaten

155g/5oz/11/2 cups Doves Farm gluten-free plain flour, sifted together with 1 teaspoon bicarbonate of soda and a good pinch of sea salt

200ml/7fl.oz/3/4 cup Alpro plain probiotic soy yoghurt

55g/2oz/1/3 cup sultanas

Finely grated rind of 1 unwaxed orange

1 tablespoon freshly chopped rosemary

55g/2oz/1/2 cup chopped walnuts

•• You will need 2 mini muffin tins lined with 24 non-stick mini muffin paper cases.

•• Preheat the oven to 200C/400F/Gas 6.

1) Put the sunflower spread and sugar into a bowl and cream them together until pale and fluffy.

2) Add the egg, some of the flour, bicarbonate of soda and salt mixture.

3) Fold in the yoghurt, followed by the remaining flour mixture.

4) Add the sultanas, finely grated orange rind, rosemary and walnuts and fold into the mixture.

5) Spoon the muffin mixture into the paper cases and bake for about 15 minutes or until golden and firm.

6) Cool a little on a wire rack and eat warm or store in an airtight container for a couple of days.

CROÛTONS

These are small, crisp golden cubes of white bread which are fried in a little oil and then served with soups and salads. The better the quality and flavour of the bread the better the croûtons. In general I would suggest that you never use rye bread but there is one brand, The Authentic Bread Company, who make a very pale and light rye bread in an 800g/1¾lb loaf. This works really well as long as it is fresh. See www.authenticbread.co.uk – this is for wheat-free croûtons only. Makes enough for 4 bowls of soup or 2 large salads

2 large thick slices (2cm/¾ in deep) of gluten-free white loaf (see stockists)

2 tablespoons of olive oil with 1 tablespoon of sunflower, vegetable, walnut or other nut oil

1) Remove the crusts and discard. Slice the bread into about seven fingers and cut into neat little cubes.
2) Put the oil into the pan and heat over medium high heat until the fat is hot enough to make the edges of the bread cubes sizzle when added. At this point add all the croûtons and fry until pale gold and crisp. Do not over-brown the croûtons or they will be rock hard and non-absorbent in the soup.
3) Place a few layers of absorbent kitchen paper on a plate and carefully lift the croûtons out with a slotted spoon.
4) Drain them on the paper and then serve them either in a warm dish or sprinkle over the soup or salads.

SMOKED SALMON BREAKFAST CUPCAKES

I had never heard of savoury cupcakes until the other day, I love savoury muffins so I thought I would try them. They make a nice change from gluten-free breads for breakfast or brunch. Makes about 12

165g/5^1/2oz/1 + ^{1}/3 cups Doves Farm gluten-free plain flour, sifted

55g/2oz/^{1}/4 cup instant polenta

1 teaspoon gluten-free baking powder

1 peeled carrot, grated

^{1}/4 teaspoon sea salt and freshly ground black pepper

A sprinkling of cayenne pepper

55g/2oz Parmazano dairy-free hard cheese (see stockists) or either goats' or pecorino cheese, finely grated

1 very small bunch fresh coriander, chopped

1 teaspoon ground coriander

200ml/7fl.oz/^{3}/4 cup unsweetened dairy-free soya milk

125ml/^{1}/4 pint/^{1}/2 cup sunflower oil

1 large egg, beaten

225g/8oz tub Tofutti Sour Supreme (dairy-free cream cheese dip) or Creamy Smooth mixed with some soya cream or milk until soft

A sprinkling of Drossa Tzatziki Herb Mix (see stockists)

12 x 10cm/4in long x 2.5cm/1in wide smoked salmon strips

•• Preheat the oven to 190C/375F/Gas 5.
•• Line a 12-hole muffin tin with cupcake cases.

1) Mix the flour, polenta, baking powder, carrot, salt and pepper, cayenne pepper, cheese, fresh and ground coriander together in a bowl. In another bowl whisk the soya milk, oil and egg together.

2) Add the wet ingredients to the dry, mixing as little as possible so that it is a lumpy batter.

3) Spoon into the prepared cases and bake in the oven for 20 minutes or until golden and firm to touch.

4) Remove from the oven and leave to cool for about 15 minutes. Meanwhile, in a small bowl combine the creamy dip with enough soya milk or cream to soften. Add enough of the tzatziki powder to taste and spread a thick swirl of the creamy mixture over the top of each cupcake.

5) Take the strips of salmon and roll each one up, teasing out the top edge as you go and you will magically have 12 roses. Place on each cupcake and serve.

PASTRY

Lots of people I meet are frightened of making pastry and they buy it which is fine if you are able to eat wheat and gluten but a disaster if you cannot. Unfortunately, pastry is one of the few skills that really do need to be taught step by step and practiced. It then becomes a cheap and easy way to feed people; from a simple shortcrust to a melting, feather-light wisp of French sweet pastry.

You do need to be confident and bold when making pastry but at the same time you must be light-handed and not over handle the pastry otherwise it can be too warm or too solid and heavy.

There are so many types of pastry but I have never been able to make a good enough gluten-free puff pastry or British hot-water crust pastry. So I will stick to the most successful ones; shortcrust, sweet pastry and choux pastry.

The first pastry to master is shortcrust pastry because it is used the most and once this pastry has been mastered then classic French pastries or flaky and puff pastry will also be easy to learn.

Shortcrust means just that, the pastry is easily crumbled so the shorter it is the crumblier it is.

In wheat flour pastries the best flour is plain flour, some recipes use self raising flour in part but the more of this you add the more "cakey" the texture is. The pastry turns out softer and less crisp than with plain flour. The gluten-free mix flours that are available vary enormously in texture and taste. The plain flours available can be made up from such varied ingredients which affect not only the taste but the texture too. Some flours are quite gritty, some very grey when baked, some too dry and some too wet. So I am going to use Doves Farm gluten-free flour mix throughout the recipes. If you use other brands you will have to experiment with the amounts of added water according to how absorbent your brand is. The best self raising flour I have come across is made by Orgran and is extremely light to work with and leaves a good aftertaste. As we are making gluten-free pastries we cannot use rye, barley or oat flours so we have to stick to rice flour and cornflour which are easily available in supermarkets. I have also found that by using Doves Farm gluten-free white bread flour you can make very light pastries.

Shortcrust pastry

To make pastry you need a combination of flour, fats, liquid and either salt or other savoury flavourings or sugar and other sweet flavourings.

The choice of fat will determine the flavour as well as the texture of the pastry. One fat can be used which will give the pastry a distinctive flavour and texture or a combination can be used.

- All butter (you could use goats') has the crispest and richest flavour but it is a little harder to rub in.

- All margarine and dairy-free spreads are slightly flakier and you need to use block or chilled fats and not soft warm margarine or spreads.

- All lard makes a shorter and flakier pastry and its distinctive flavour is good for savoury pies but not so good for sweet. Lard pastry needs less water for mixing and needs to be kept cool because it reaches room temperature more quickly than butter or either margarine or spreads.

- The combination of half butter and half lard is great because it is easy to rub in and to handle. The pastry has a good texture which is crispy enough and the flavour is good for most recipes.

- The combination of half margarine or spread and half lard is also easy to rub in and to roll out and produces a less expensive and delicious pastry.

- Whichever fats you choose they should be at room temperature because if it is too cold it will take too long to rub in and if it is too warm it will be oily and with the additional heat from your hands it will be too soft to rub in.

- Liquids are usually either cold water or beaten eggs. The colder the water is the better. Quantities vary enormously because the different flours absorb different amounts. It is safer to add a little at a time so that you end up with smooth dough without any dryish bits or cracks in it. The dough should be moist enough to leave the bowl fairly clean. If you add too much water you will produce a hard crust and if you add too little it will be hard to roll out.

Shortcrust pastry tips

- Keep your kitchen cool and airy when making pastry, if this is impossible then you can use a marble pastry slab or make it direct on a granite work surface. Keep your hands cool, the water cold and the fat at room temperature for maximum success.

- You need to sift the flour into a bowl so that the flour is aerated and the fat needs to be cut into small lumps so that it is easy to rub into the flour. Start off using a round-bladed knife and cut the fat into the flour.

- When it is well mixed then start using your fingertips only. Lift the pieces of fat up and rub them gently through your fingers. Keep your hands high above the bowl and let the air and lightness in.

- At this point the less you handle the pastry the better so speed is of the essence. Start to add the water about 1 teaspoon at a time. Use the knife again to mix the dough and when it comes together use your hands to bring the dough into a ball.

- If you rest the pastry in a cool place it will help prevent it from shrinking during cooking and it will help to stop it breaking when you roll it out. It can be wrapped in cling film or foil but it must be covered so that it doesn't acquire a dry skin which will crack when you start to roll it.

- It sounds silly but a long rolling pin can really help when rolling out your pastry, the result will be more even and so try and use one that is 45cm/18in long.

- A flour dredger is not vital but a light sprinkling of flour for rolling is best. Place the dough on a lightly floured board or hard surface. The surface must be flat and clean. It is a good idea to dust the rolling pin with flour too.

- Roll the pastry quickly so that it keeps cool.

- Place your hand flat on each end of the rolling pin and roll the pastry out gently with even pressure. Dust the rolling pin each time it gets sticky. Don't turn the pastry over whilst rolling. If you are rolling a specific shape always revolve the pastry and not the rolling pin. So for a circle, keep giving the pastry a quarter-turn after each rolling. Any shape should be rolled out slightly larger than the size of the dish or tin you are using.

- To transfer the pastry to the dish you need to place the rolling pin at either end of the pastry and lightly roll the pastry around the rolling pin then carefully and quickly transfer it to the waiting dish or tin. Place the tip of the pastry over one edge of the tin and gently unroll.

- Trim off any overlapping bits that are too big to fold back into the tin and neaten the edges very gently with a blunt knife or fork. Make sure that you press the pastry well into the dish or tin so that no air gets trapped underneath.

- If you are cutting pastry shapes after rolling then you need to dust the edge of the cutter each time. Push the cutter firmly and give it a sharp tap, don't twist the cutter.

- Baking "blind" means cooking the pastry on its own in the oven before the filling is put in. If any air has got trapped beneath the pastry then this is when it will balloon up. You can line your pastry shapes with lining paper circles or whatever shape is needed and a thin layer of ceramic beans or balls.

- However, if there is no air trapped and if you prick the base with a fork you shouldn't really need these extras. The liquid filling does not run out of the holes made by the fork because during cooking the pastry sets and the holes close up.

- You can also brush the base with beaten egg which keeps the pastry crisp when the filling is added. For emergencies – if you see the pastry puffing up then just prick it with a fork and press it down gently and it will be ok.

- A good tip for baking gluten-free pastry is to put the tin onto a baking sheet or tray, this conducts the heat evenly and ensures a crisp base. Pastry needs to be cooked at a high temperature, normally ranging between 190-220C/375-425F/Gas 5-7 the highest temperature being for flaky or puff pastry.

- The last tip I have is that pastry is best cooked in metal tins as they are a better conductor of heat than porcelain or glass. Often quiches made in pretty porcelain dishes have soggy bottoms!

SHORTCRUST PASTRY

This recipe makes about 450g/1lb pastry which is enough to line any 24-28cm/9^1/2-11in tin or 4 fluted deep tartlet tins. You can use it for making any quiches, savoury pies or sweet fruit-filled pies, mince pies or tarts. Don't forget to get the fats to room temperature before using.

225g/8oz/1^3/4 cup Doves Farm gluten-
   free plain flour
A pinch of sea salt
55g/2oz dairy-free sunflower spread

55g/2oz hard white vegetable shortening
   (Trex and Cookeen are good)
1 large egg, beaten
2 tablespoons cold water

•• Preheat the oven to 180C/350F/Gas 4.

1) Hold the sieve as high as possible and sift the flour and salt into a large mixing bowl.
2) Add the sunflower spread and cut the remaining fat into small cubes and mix both into the flour with a blunt knife and then with your floured fingertips.
3) Keep your hands as high as possible to aerate the mixture. When the mixture resembles breadcrumbs, add the beaten egg and sprinkle with the water. The dough will not roll out without sticking if it is too wet, equally it will break up if too dry but practice makes perfect!
4) Mix once again with the knife. If you need more water add a teaspoon at a time until the pastry comes into a smooth ball of dough and leaves the sides of the bowl fairly clean.
5) Wrap in cling film or foil and chill for 1 hour.
6) Flour a clean board or area of your kitchen worktop. Unwrap the dough and place it in the centre of the floured area and flour your rolling pin.
7) Roll the dough into a large enough circle to line the tin or quiche dish.
8) To top a fruit pie you should cut out a circle slightly larger than the pie dish and place it over the cooked fruit. Trim off any excess pastry around the dish, seal and decorate the edges by pressing the prongs of a fork all the way round or press the end of a round ended knife into scallop shapes. Always cut a steam hole in the middle of the pastry. To glaze, brush with beaten egg and sprinkle with caster sugar and bake until golden brown.
9) For a tart, the pastry should sit loosely over the tin as you slide it carefully with the help of a palette knife. Don't attempt to use only the rolling pin as the pastry is too breakable. Gently work the pastry into the base and up the sides with floured fingers. Mending and blending where necessary. This will be fine when it is baked.
10) To finish the tart press the pastry into the flutes so that it rises above the tin as this will help prevent too much shrinkage. Lightly slice off the edges and discard trimmings. Prick the base with a fork in a few places and then follow your chosen recipe.
11) For a tart or a pie: Bake in the centre of the oven for about 35 minutes until the pastry is cooked through and golden.

SWEET TART OR PIE PASTRY

There are some delicious French sweet pastry recipes such as pâte brisée and pâte sucrée but as the techniques are pretty advanced I have decided to use a sweet English pastry. You can use this recipe for mince pies, fruit pies or treacle tart. Makes 23cm/9in fluted tart base or 1 pie cover

200g/7oz/1 1/2 cups Doves Farm gluten-
    free plain flour, extra for dusting
55g/2oz/scant 1/2 cup sifted icing sugar
Pinch of sea salt

100g/3 1/2 oz dairy-free sunflower spread
1 large egg
Suggested glaze for fruit pies: water or
    beaten egg and caster sugar

•• Preheat the oven to 180C/350F/Gas 4.
•• You will need baking parchment and baking balls or beans.

1) Put all the pastry ingredients together into a food processor and pulse briefly until the mixture forms crumbs and then gathers into lumps or a ball of dough.
2) Carefully remove the dough, dust with flour, wrap in cling film and chill for about 30 minutes.
3) Flour a clean board or area of your kitchen worktop. Place the dough in the centre of the floured area and flour your rolling pin.
4) Roll the dough into a large enough circle to line the tin. For a tart the pastry should sit loosely over the tin as you slide it carefully with the help of a palette knife or rolling pin. Don't attempt to use the rolling pin if it is too crumbly. Gently work the pastry into the base and up the sides with floured fingers. Mending and blending where necessary. This will be fine when it is baked.
5) To finish the tart press the pastry into the flutes so that it rises above the tin as this will help prevent too much shrinkage. Lightly slice off the edges with a sharp knife and discard trimmings. Prick the base with a fork in a few places and then bake blind (see page 118) for 10 minutes. Remove the baking parchment and baking beans/balls and bake for a further 10 minutes. Fill immediately and bake according to instructions or follow your chosen recipe.
6) For a pie you should cut out a circle slightly larger than the pie dish and place it over the cooked fruit. For best effect cut any shapes or borders to edge the dish and brush with water to attach the decorations or borders to the pastry. Trim off any excess pastry around the dish and always cut a steam hole in the middle of the pastry. To glaze the pastry, brush it with beaten egg and sprinkle with caster sugar and bake until golden brown.

CHOUX PASTRY

Choux pastry is a light and airy pastry which is used to make éclairs, profiteroles or savoury gougères. It puffs up in a very hot oven until the heat sets the pastry. The high water content of the pastry produces steam which forces the pastry to puff outwards and gives it volume. Lots of recipes call for piping the pastry into buns or éclairs but so much of the mixture sticks to the inside of the bag that I recommend simply spooning the mixture into bun or log shapes. This is a much easier and quicker way to make the recipe and can also help the choux pastry to look crustier. Choux pastry doesn't improve with keeping so eat within 4-8 hours if possible and avoid filling more than a couple of hours in advance if you are going to make a gluten or dairy-free crème pâtisserie as the pastry will become soggy.

If you use the best quality dark chocolate it will more than make up for not using fresh cream. You don't have to be good at making pastry to make profiteroles or éclairs because you are not using your hands which can sometimes be too hot or heavy handed. Neither do you need a rolling pin which can be under-floured and cause sticky pastry or which can be used over vigorously leading to tough pastry.

The most brilliant thing about this recipe is that it needs to be made in a food processor or with an electric hand whisk. This makes choux pastry with great speed and ease and with predictable results every time.

PROFITEROLES WITH CHOCOLATE SAUCE

This recipe should make about 16-18 profiteroles but you can easily make double and there will be enough ice cream and chocolate sauce to serve 8-10 people. Serves 4-6

Profiteroles
125ml/^{1}/4 pint/^{1}/2 cup water
55g/2oz/^{1}/4 cup dairy-free sunflower spread
70g/2^1/2oz/^{1}/2 cup Doves Farm gluten-free plain flour
2 large eggs

Filling
^{1}/2 x 750ml/1^1/4 pint tub Swedish Glace Vanilla or Rich Chocolate ice cream
Chocolate sauce recipe page 47

•• Preheat the oven to 200C/400F/Gas 6.

1) Line a baking tray with baking parchment.
2) Put the water in a pan with the sunflower spread. Bring the mixture to the boil, remove pan from the heat and tip the flour into the boiling water.
3) Immediately beat with an electric hand whisk until the mix comes away from the side of the pan. Cool the dough slightly and transfer to a bowl.
4) Gradually add the eggs, beating with the electric hand whisk until it is smooth and shiny.
5) Take heaped teaspoonfuls of the choux pastry and place each one at intervals on the prepared baking tray. The profiteroles will become puffy and well risen so leave some space between each one. You should make about 16 in all.
6) Bake for about 20-25 minutes or until golden but do not open the oven door before about 20 minutes or they might collapse.
7) Meanwhile, make the chocolate sauce.
8) Quickly put the cooked profiteroles onto a wire rack and slice each one in half horizontally or half the way across if preferred. If there is any uncooked dough inside a profiterole it is best to gently pull it out with your finger tips to prevent the whole bun becoming soggy.
9) Just before serving take the ice cream out of the deep freeze so it is soft enough to scoop straight away. Fill the base of each profiterole with the ice cream, top with the remaining half, arrange on a plate in a mountain and drizzle over the chocolate sauce. Serve the rest of the sauce in a warm jug.

CAKES AND COOKIES

It is well worth acquiring a small repertoire of cakes and cookies because it is a very easy and cheap way of entertaining. A slice of cake and a cup of tea is very relaxing with a friend, while full on afternoon tea is very popular with all ages. Not only this but lots of parents and children can be exhausting and expensive for lunch but tea is ideal for most age groups.

Even the simplest of cookies melt in the mouth and the plainest of cakes are generally far better in taste, texture, colour and smell than shop bought cakes. But lets be frank here, this is all about pleasure and indulgence, comfort and special treats and not about nutrition! This means that you can splash out on the best ingredients. Organic free-range eggs, unrefined sugar, jam full of fruit and high cocoa content chocolate will all combine to make fantastic tea-time treats.

Basic Cake-Making Hints

Measurements
Baking is one area of cooking where it is vital to have measurements 100% accurate. The ratio of sugar to butter/dairy-free spreads to eggs to flour is vital for success. This is one area where improvisation seldom works. The icing and the fillings you can play around with a bit more freely.

Cake tins
The most important thing about a cake tin is not how new it is or its shape but that it is the right size for the recipe. Just 2.5cm/1in will make all the difference. If the tin is too big your mixture will be too crusty and biscuity instead of light and plump. If the tin is too small the mixture will take longer to cook and so is more likely to burn on top well before the inside is set. So make sure that you have enough of the right size tins before starting on home baking.

I always line cake tins with baking parchment even if the tin is non-stick because in the end it is so much easier this way than risking leaving a small lump of cake sticking to the base of the tin.

Preparing to bake a cake
This sounds ridiculously obvious but the oven must be pre-heated so that the correct temperature is reached when the cake is put into the oven or it will not rise and it will be heavy and stodgy. This gives you time to get all your ingredients ready and then to prepare the cake tin.

Take your cake tin and very lightly grease it with your chosen fat. I suggest clean fingers as the easiest option but you can use a thick piece of folded baking parchment or a wad of kitchen paper.

You can then dust it lightly with flour or you can cut a circle of baking parchment to fit the tin, place it on the greased surface and then dust the sides and any gaps with suitable flour.

As a word of advice don't buy greaseproof paper instead of baking paper/parchment as it is not the same thing at all. I suggest unrolling a good length of the paper and drawing circles on a flat surface so that it is easy to cut out and not all wonky and wobbly! If you are in the mood or can get children to do this for you why not make a dozen and then you can save time when you are busier.

Nowadays there are fantastic Teflon-based pre-cut baking sheets available in the shops. I am a great fan of them because you simply use, wash and wipe clean and put away for another time, saving all the repeated cutting out time.

Methods of cake making

Generally there are two traditional ways of making a cake. The creamed method is where you beat the butter/dairy-free spread and sugar together for a light traditional sponge. The alternative is to whisk egg yolks and sugar together, whisking and folding in the egg whites to make the finest and lightest of cakes. There are other methods such as mixing oil with sugar and carrots for a carrot cake or the cheating method which I will come to.

The aim when you are making a cake is to create a structure which can incorporate as much air as possible in the batter. This will ensure a light cake and not a stodgy dense cake. As it bakes the bubbles of air expand and the cake rises perfectly.

The cheating method is acceptable for emergencies but does not give this light airy result. The cheat is that the cake is made all-in-one in a bowl. You save time on the preparation and the washing up by putting all the ingredients together in a bowl. Extra baking powder is needed to help the cake rise and then you simply beat the mixture until soft and smooth. Fruit cakes are pretty good made this way. You can also make cakes in the Magimix/food processor as long as you don't over beat them.

Creaming method

Use softened butter or dairy-free spread to make creaming easier. Put the fat in a mixing bowl with the sugar and mash them together with a wooden spoon. Once the mixture is blended then beat the cake mixture with a wooden spoon and with plenty of vigour. The mixture should be light and fluffy and the granules of sugar should no longer be visible. This means that you have successfully dissolved the sugar into the fat which brings the air into the mixture. You can use an electric hand mixer for speedier results.

Whisking method

Put the whole eggs or egg yolks as the recipe instructs you into a mixing bowl with the sugar and whisk together with a balloon whisk or for speedier results with an electric hand whisk. Don't stop until the mixture is very pale and thick. You can test if the batter is thick enough by lifting up the whisk (don't forget to turn the electric whisk off first or you and your surfaces will be covered in batter droplets). Then wave the whisk gently around a few times into a figure of 8 over the cake mixture and if the definition of the 8 disappears instantly then you know it is not thick enough. If the 8 remains visible on the surface the batter is perfectly blended and so the sugar is dissolved and sufficient air is incorporated.

Whisked egg white method

In some recipes like the Austrian Sachertorte for example, the egg yolks and sugar are creamed to make a batter. Once all the ingredients are incorporated the egg whites are whisked to the soft peak stage and folded into the cake mixture. It is very important to stir in one spoonful of the whisked whites into the mixture first to slacken it. This will make it easier to fold in the remaining whites but also will help prevent breaking down the bulk of the egg whites.

As before, aim to get as much air as possible into the batter, always use a metal spoon as this crushes out less air than a wooden or plastic one. As with meringues slide the edge of the spoon down into the whites and cake mixture, to the bottom of the bowl and then bring the spoon up and through the mixture and back on top of itself. Keep repeating this action working fast but carefully until the whites are completely incorporated into the batter with no visible white lumps flecking the mixture.

Dropping consistency
Most cakes need a batter that is of dropping consistency. This means that the batter drops off the spoon easily when the spoon is tapped on the side of the mixing bowl. Too stiff will make the cakes rather solid and too runny will take too long to set and even worse may leak out of a tin with a loose base.

Baking the cake
As well as preheating the oven, check that the shelves are in the right place too. The cake should sit in the centre of the oven so that it will cook evenly. Too close to the sides or top of the oven will leave you with burnt edges or top. Slide the cake carefully into the oven and always set your oven timer to 5 minutes less than specified in the recipe in case your oven is hotter. For a fruit cake I would do this 20 minutes before as the cooking times are much longer. This will mean that you won't be tempted to check the cake way before it is cooked, and risk that sinking experience! If, in your experience, one side of the cake tends to cook more than the other, turn the cake round for more even cooking. If the tops tend to burn then place a layer of baking parchment loosely over the top for sponge cakes or foil for fruit cakes.

Cooking the cake
When you bring the cake out of the oven check that the surface is golden and well risen. Then you can test that it is fully cooked by carefully and very briefly touching the centre of the cake with your finger tips. It should feel firm, the dip should bounce back quickly and the edges should be pulling away from the sides of the tin. If the cake is not baked through then return it very quickly to the oven for 5-10 minutes.

For a fruit cake or very dense carrot or chocolate cake you can check by inserting a skewer into the centre of the cake and if it comes out clean and dry it is certainly cooked. If the skewer is coated in mixture quickly return the cake to the oven for another 20 minutes. Not forgetting to cover loosely with foil if you think it may catch.

Turning out the cake
Never turn the cake out straight from the oven as it could sink or worse, collapse!

Leave the cake in its tin on a wire rack for about 20 minutes to firm up. Very large cakes, fruit or dense chocolate or carrot cakes will need about an hour. Some very fragile cakes may need to cool completely but follow the guides in the recipe.

Run a blunt ended knife around the cake tin sides, keeping it very close so as not to cut into the cake. Turn the cake carefully onto a wire rack to cool. Peel off baking parchment or Teflon sheets so that the cake can breathe and cool down more quickly.

When the cake is cold you can transfer the bottom half onto a plate ready to fill or if the cake needs slicing in half you can do this now. Carefully place the top cake over the filling so that it doesn't look wonky. The cake is then ready to ice and decorate or dust with other ingredients in your recipe. If you try and fill the cake when it is still warm the filling will soften and the top sponge will literally slide off! Any icing will also slide off a warm cake.

Little tips:
- Gradually add a little beaten egg at a time to your cake mixture to help prevent curdling. Add a little flour to stabilize it and then continue to add the beaten egg. Curdling is not the end of the world but the cake will not rise as much if it does curdle.

- It is always good to keep a lemon in the kitchen; the zest is great to flavour a sponge and the juice for a butter cream filling or the icing. It has an alchemy of its own too as it always seems to help with raising sponges and fairy cakes.

- Dusting cakes is a good way of reducing sugar intake. It is also a marvellous reduction in the time taken in preparing and icing with glacé, royal or frosted icing and of course there is practically no washing up. Simply use a small fine sieve, shake a little icing sugar over the top of the cake at the last minute.

As you can probably imagine there are so many wonderful cake recipes around that I found it very difficult to choose such a small selection. Here are my favourites and some fun cakes for my lovely little daughter who won't eat any biscuits but loves cakes to distraction!

CHRISTMAS OR BIRTHDAY CAKE

This is the cake that I have made for the past two Christmases and made recently for a special birthday party. You can halve the quantities for a much smaller cake, using 3 eggs. Serves about 16-20

750g/1lb 10oz/5 cups mixed fruit with citrus peel (sultanas, raisins and currants)

250g/9oz/1³/4 cups dried, soft juicy apricot halves, coarsely chopped

200g/7oz/2 cups dried, soft juicy peach halves, coarsely chopped

175g/6oz/³/4 cup natural glacé cherries, halved

125g/4¹/2oz /1 cup dried, soft juicy pears, coarsely chopped

Grated zest and juice of 1 large unwaxed orange

200ml/7fl.oz/³/4 cup brandy plus extra for topping up cake

3 teaspoons ground allspice

100g/3¹/2oz/1 cup walnut pieces, roughly chopped

4 whole stem ginger in syrup, finely chopped

250g/8oz dairy-free sunflower spread

200g/7oz/1¹/2 cups dark muscovado (soft dark brown) sugar

5 large eggs, beaten

300g/11oz/2 + ¹/3 cups Doves Farm gluten-free plain flour, sieved

3 tablespoons reduced sugar apricot jam

270g/10oz pack of Dr. Oetker ready rolled Regalice white icing, or make your own

270g/10oz pack of marzipan (check it is gluten free) – use double if you like a thick layer of marzipan

Extra icing sugar for dusting and your chosen decorations

- 24x8cm/9¹/2x3in round/deep cake tin, greased and sides and base lined with non-stick baking parchment.
- Preheat the oven to 170C/325F/Gas 3.

1) One day in advance, place all the fruit in a very large bowl with the orange juice and zest and the brandy. Add the spice, nuts and chopped ginger and mix in. Keep covered and cool while it soaks.

2) Beat together the sunflower spread with the sugar until smooth and creamy.

3) Beat in half the egg and then half the flour and repeat until used up.

4) Spoon the mixture into the prepared tin and bake for about 3-4 hours or until the cake is firm to touch. Cover loosely with foil if the top browns too much. An inserted skewer should come out clean and not clinging with wet mixture.

5) Leave the cake to get cold in the tin. Turn it out onto a wire rack keeping the lining paper on and wrap the cake tightly in foil or leave in a sealed container to mature. Every few weeks feed the cake by making small holes with a skewer in its top and then drizzling with more brandy. This keeps the cake moist.

6) Put the cake onto a serving plate. If it is domed you can slice off the hump and turn the cake upside down to ice it.

7) In a small pan warm the jam with 1 tablespoon cold water and then brush the cake all over.

8) Dust a clean surface with icing sugar, keep dusting the rolling pin as you roll out the marzipan thinly into a circle to cover your cake and down the sides. If you like very thick marzipan then you should combine two packets. Lift the marzipan over the cake and then ease it down the sides. Trim off any excess and seal any gaps. Cover with cling film for 2 days before icing.

9) Remove the cling film and brush the marzipan lightly with water. Follow the instructions on the pack of rolled icing to completely cover your cake, smooth it carefully down the sides and seal it. Trim off any excess icing from around the base.

10) When the icing is set decorate with ribbons and candles or make or buy your Christmas decorations.

FROSTED CARROT CAKE

This is my all time favourite carrot cake. It is so quick and easy in the Magimix /food processor that I have actually been making it for 25 years. Others that I have tried have been too dry or too heavy and simply lacking the delicious generosity of fruits, spices and carrots. Serves 12-16

250g/8oz organic carrots, peeled

227g/8oz can pineapple chunks in fruit juice, drained

2 medium eggs

175g/6oz/scant cup caster sugar

250ml/9fl.oz/1 cup vegetable oil

1 tablespoon lemon or orange juice

175g/6oz/1^1/2 cups Orgran self raising gluten-free flour

^{1}/2 teaspoon bicarbonate of soda

^{1}/4 teaspoon of sea salt

1 tablespoon gluten-free baking powder

1 teaspoon ground cinnamon

A good dusting of freshly grated nutmeg

1 teaspoon of allspice

55g/2oz/^{1}/2 cup walnut pieces, chopped

Topping

125g/4^1/2oz dairy-free sunflower spread

225g/8oz tub Tofutti creamy smooth dairy-free original (see stockists)

2 teaspoons pure vanilla extract

115-140g/4-5oz/^{3}/4-1 cup icing sugar, according to taste

•• You will need a 23cm/9in non-stick spring-release, loose bottomed cake tin.
•• Preheat the oven to 180C/350F/Gas 4.

1) Cut the carrots to fit the Magimix/food processor feed tube lengthwise.
2) Fit the fine grating disc, grate the carrots and reserve.
3) Fit the double-bladed knife. Drain the pineapple, put in the bowl and whiz for a few seconds until chopped but not mush. Remove and reserve.
4) Return the bowl and blade to the Magimix/ food processor and break the eggs into it with the sugar and beat until well mixed. Keep the motor on and slowly pour the oil in through the feed tube. Process until smooth and thick and add the lemon juice.
5) Add the flour and other dry ingredients and briefly process until mixed in.
6) Add the carrot, pineapple and walnuts and pulse the machine a few times until the mixture is evenly distributed.
7) Turn the cake mixture into the prepared tin and bake for about 1^1/4 hours until firm to touch on the top.
8) Leave to cool for an hour in the tin, turn out onto a wire rack.
9) Make the topping using a clean processor blade and bowl.
10) Put the sunflower spread, cream cheese-style spread and vanilla in a bowl and mix until smooth. Sift in the icing sugar and stir until smooth. The more sugar you put in the runnier the topping will be.
11) When the cake is cold, spread the topping over the top of the cake.

•• Keep cool or refrigerate until needed.

VICTORIA SPONGE

This is as traditional as a cake gets and is loved by all ages and generations.
My grandmother filled hers with raspberry jam but I always fill mine with strawberry jam
and whipped cream. This is also a very good birthday cake if you double the quantities and
use bigger tins. Fill with layers of jam, whipped cream, sliced strawberries or raspberries
and then ice in any colour/s you like and decorate. For a dairy-free birthday cake I assemble
it at the very last minute using Swedish Glace vanilla ice cream, dust the cake with sifted
icing sugar and decorate it with sparklers and candles. Serves 8

175g/6oz dairy-free sunflower spread
175g/6oz/1 scant cup caster sugar
3 large eggs, beaten
200g/7oz/1¾ cups Orgran gluten-free self
  raising flour

1 teaspoon gluten-free baking powder
Raspberry or strawberry jam
Icing sugar, sifted

•• Preheat the oven to 180C/350F/Gas 4.
•• Base-line two 23cm/9in cake tins with baking parchment.

1) Cream the sunflower spread with the sugar in a mixing bowl until light and fluffy using a
   wooden spoon.
2) Beat in a spoonful of the egg at a time until about half is incorporated – this will prevent the
   mixture from curdling.
3) Mix one tablespoon of the flour into the mixture and then continue with the beaten egg.
4) Fold in the remaining flour and the baking powder. If the batter is not of dropping consistency
   then add in a tablespoon of hot water.
5) Divide the mixture between the two prepared tins and shake slightly to smooth and even the
   tops. Never press the tops with the back of the spoon or it will flatten the sponge.
6) Bake for about 25 minutes or until the cake is golden and the top is firm and springs back
   when touched with fingertips. Cool for 10 minutes in the tin and then turn them out onto a
   wire rack.
7) When the cakes are cold sandwich them together on a serving plate with the jam and dust
   with sifted icing sugar.

WICKED CHOCOLATE CAKE

A double hit of chocolate is naturally more chocolatey and wickedly indulgent but it doesn't have to be sweeter hence the need for some cocoa powder and high cocoa content chocolate. The percentage of cocoa is marked on all good quality bars of chocolate and the higher the better. I suggest 50% as your lowest figure and 80% as your highest. Serves 8-10

115g/4oz Kinnerton Luxury Dark
   Chocolate, broken into squares
200g/7oz/scant 2 cups Doves Farm gluten-
   free plain flour
30g/1oz dairy-free cocoa powder
3 level teaspoons gluten-free baking
   powder
175g/6oz dairy-free sunflower spread
60g/2^{1}/2oz/^{1}/2 cup soft brown sugar
115g/4oz/^{1}/2 cup caster sugar

4 large eggs, separated
3 tablespoons unsweetened dairy-free
   soya milk

Filling and Icing
200g/7oz Kinnerton Luxury Dark
   Chocolate, broken into squares
175ml/6fl.oz/^{3}/4 cup soya dairy-free single
   cream
225g/8oz/2 cups icing sugar

•• Preheat the oven to 180C/350F/Gas 4.

1) Grease and base-line two 20cm/8in shallow cake tins.
2) Melt the chocolate in a heatproof bowl set over a pan of simmering water. Lift the bowl off the pan, stir the chocolate, leave to cool until tepid.
3) Sift the flour with the cocoa and baking powder into a mixing bowl.
4) Cream the sunflower spread in a large mixing bowl with both the sugars. Beat in the melted chocolate and then the egg yolks, one at a time.
5) Fold in one third of the flour followed by 1 tablespoon soya milk. Repeat until all of the flour and soya milk have been used up.
6) In a large clean bowl, preferably metal or glass, whisk the egg whites with an electric hand whisk until they form soft peaks. Beat a tablespoon of the egg whites into the chocolate mixture and fold the remainder in lightly with a metal spoon.
7) Divide the mixture between the two cake tins and level off with a shake or two. Bake them in the oven for 25 minutes or until just firm. Test with an inserted skewer. Never press down the mixture with the back of a wooden spoon or the cake will not rise.
8) Leave the cakes to cool in their tins for about 20 minutes, then turn the cakes out and leave until cold on a wire rack.
9) Meanwhile, you can make the filling and icing. Melt the chocolate in a heatproof bowl, refer to full instructions on page 143, over a pan of simmering water. Warm the cream through in a small pan which will prevent the icing from setting too quickly.
10) As soon as the chocolate is smooth, remove the bowl from the heat and gradually beat in the cream. Sift the icing sugar and beat it into the chocolate until you have a smooth fudgy mixture.
11) Sandwich together the two cakes on a serving plate with one third of the chocolate mixture. Spread the rest over the top and sides. It looks great if you rough it up a bit with the end of a fork. You can finish the cake off with a little grated chocolate if you like.

•• Store in a cool place in a sealed container for up to 2 days before needed.

ORANGE AND ALMOND CAKE

This recipe is one of the few naturally gluten-free recipes I have come across. As it is flourless it has a dense but moist texture and is certainly very orangey.

The cake keeps for 3 days so you can prepare well ahead for parties. The usual dry-knife test won't work here because the cake is too moist so to test when it is cooked simply tap the edge of the cake. It is ready when it no longer wobbles in the middle. Serves 8

4 large unwaxed oranges
200g/7oz/1 cup caster sugar
200g/7oz/2¼ cups ground almonds

1 heaped teaspoon gluten-free baking
  powder
6 medium eggs
Apricot or orange jam

•• Preheat the oven to 180C/350F/Gas 4.
•• You will need a 23cm/9in spring-form cake tin lined with baking parchment.

1) Put the oranges in a pan and cover with boiling water. Bring to the boil, turn down the heat and simmer for 2 hours.
2) Top up with more water as they start to boil dry. Take off the heat and leave to cool.
3) Remove the oranges from the water and cut two into quarters discarding the pips or hard bits. Place these two oranges in a food processor with the remaining ingredients and briefly blitz until smooth and well mixed.
4) Thickly slice the remaining cooked oranges and arrange over the base of the cake tin. Just use the best slices and discard the rest.
5) Spoon the mixture over the oranges, lightly smoothing over the top.
6) Bake for 1½ hours, covering the cake with foil half-way through if necessary (if the top is browning too fast).
7) Leave the cake to cool in the tin and when cold turn it out onto a plate. Brush the top of the cake and oranges with melted apricot or orange jam to give it a nice glaze.
8) Serve the cake on its own or with dairy-free vanilla ice cream. You can store it in an airtight container for up to 3 days.

BANANA CAKE

This is the best banana cake that I have ever made and I think it is due to the fact the amount of banana used is weighed. This is because a ripe banana and an unripe banana weigh different amounts and as the recipe calls for the sweetness of ripe bananas it is far better to have an exact amount. Use bananas that have lots of black spots that no one else wants to eat! I have omitted nuts because most recipes seemed to have them and I have given the cake an orange icing instead of the more widely used lemon flavour. Serves 6

225g/8oz ripe banana, mashed weight
Juice 1 large lemon
1 teaspoon pure vanilla extract
225g/8oz/2 cups Doves Farm gluten-free plain flour, sifted
1 teaspoon baking powder
1/2 teaspoon bicarbonate of soda
115g/4oz dairy-free sunflower spread

140g/5oz/1 cup light muscovado sugar
2 medium eggs, beaten
4 tablespoons soya dairy-free single cream
To ice the cake mix some sifted icing sugar with a little fresh zest and juice of a large unwaxed orange until thick and smooth

•• You will need a 20x13cm/8x5in non-stick loaf tin lined with baking parchment.
•• Preheat the oven to 180C/350F/Gas 4.

1) Peel the banana/s, break into pieces in a bowl and mash with a fork until smooth. Stir in the lemon juice and the vanilla.
2) In another bowl mix the flour with the baking powder and bicarbonate of soda.
3) In a large mixing bowl beat the sunflower spread with the sugar with a balloon whisk until soft and pale. Whisk in half the egg at a time.
4) Lightly stir in the mashed banana and soya cream. Gently fold in the flour mixture with a metal spoon half at a time.
5) Spoon the mixture into the tin and bake for about 40-50 minutes. The cake should be golden, well risen, firm to the touch but still moist in the centre.
6) Leave the cake in the tin for 20 minutes. Loosen the sides with a round-bladed knife before turning out onto a wire rack. Peel off the lining paper and leave to cool completely.
7) The cake will keep for 3 days in an airtight container. Ice the cake before serving by mixing some sifted icing sugar in a bowl with a little orange juice and zest. I leave the quantities to you as some people prefer a drizzle of icing and some like lashings. The icing needs to be thick and smooth.

GINGER AND CHOCOLATE COOKIES

I have tried many cookie recipes over the years and most of them are far too sweet for me but this cookie mix with the hint of ginger helps to make the cookie a bit more sophisticated. For kids simply exclude the ginger and add chopped nuts or ready-to-eat dried berries or raisins. Makes 24 cookies

150g/5oz/3/4 cup caster sugar

150g/5oz dairy-free sunflower spread

225g/8oz/2 cups Doves Farm gluten-free plain flour, sifted

3 level teaspoons gluten-free baking powder

1 tablespoon unsweetened dairy-free soya milk

115g/4oz Kinnerton Luxury Dark Chocolate, chopped

5 x whole preserved ginger from a jar, drained and chopped

•• Preheat the oven to 180C/350F/Gas 4.

1) Grease 2 large baking sheets with a little extra spread and line with baking parchment.
2) Beat together the sugar and sunflower spread in a large mixing bowl until pale and creamy.
3) Stir in the remaining ingredients until you have a soft dough. Use a metal spoon to scoop a walnut sized piece of dough onto the prepared baking sheet. (By this I mean a whole walnut shell.)
4) Space them out generously. The cookies will spread quite a lot and you will need to cook them in several batches. I usually manage 6 at a time.
5) Use a fork to gently press each ball down to form a rough disc about 1cm/1/2 inch thick.
6) Bake for about 10 minutes until a pale gold colour and still soft in the middle. Swap the trays round half way through cooking time so that they cook evenly.
7) Leave on the baking sheets for 10 minutes and then transfer onto wire racks to cool otherwise they will crumble and break.

FLOURLESS CHOCOLATE BROWNIES

For best results make these brownies the day before they are needed. Keep them overnight in the tin. There are so many recipes for brownies but over the years I have used maybe a couple that have been perfect. Some have been too gooey and others too hard or too sweet. These are just right and delicious with vanilla dairy-free ice cream as a pudding. Serves 8

225g/8oz Kinnerton Luxury Dark Chocolate

225g/8oz dairy-free sunflower spread

2 teaspoons pure vanilla extract

200g/7oz/1 cup caster sugar

3 large eggs, beaten

150g/5oz/1 1/2 cups ground almonds

100g/3 1/2 oz/1 cup roughly chopped walnuts

•• You will need a 20x30cm/ 8x12in rectangular non-stick baking tin, lined with non-stick baking paper.

•• Preheat the oven to 170C/325F/Gas 3.

1) In a large thick-based saucepan, melt the chocolate with the sunflower spread gently over very low heat.
2) Remove the pan from the heat, mix in the vanilla and sugar, stir until smooth and cool a little.
3) Beat in the eggs followed by the ground almonds and walnuts. Pour the mixture into the prepared tin and bake in the oven for about 35 minutes.
4) The brownie should be firm and set on top but gooey in the middle. Cool for a few hours and then cut into 12 squares. When the brownies are completely cold you can carefully slide the set of brownies in the paper onto a flat surface.
5) Cut each brownie in half to make 24 small ones as they are extremely rich. Lift them off the paper and serve with dairy-free ice cream or just as they are. If there are any left, store them in an airtight container until needed but keep them in a cool place.

DORSET APPLE CAKE

There are lots of versions of this cake but this is rather a good vanilla one. You can change the sponge flavour to lemon by substituting the vanilla for lemon juice and adding the zest of one unwaxed lemon. Serves 8

450g/1lb eating apples
Juice of 1/2 lemon
225g/8oz dairy-free sunflower spread
225g/8oz/1 heaped cup caster sugar
2 teaspoons pure vanilla extract
3 large eggs

225g/8oz/2 cups Orgran gluten-free self raising flour, sifted
2 teaspoons gluten-free baking powder
30g/1oz/1/3 heaped cup ground almonds
1 tablespoon demerara sugar

•• You will need a deep 20cm/8in spring-form cake tin lined with baking paper.
•• Preheat the oven to 180C/350F/Gas 4.

1) Peel, core and cut the apples into thick slices. Chop them into 50 pence-sized pieces and toss with the lemon juice in a bowl.
2) Cream the sunflower spread together with the sugar and vanilla in a large bowl until creamy and fluffy using a wooden spoon.
3) Beat in the eggs one at a time, adding a little flour each time to help keep the mixture smooth.
4) Fold in the remaining flour, the baking powder and ground almonds. Fold in the apples with a metal spoon and distribute evenly.
5) Spoon the mixture into the prepared tin and sprinkle with the demerara sugar. Bake the cake for 35 minutes, it will be firm and golden on top. Cover the cake loosely with foil and bake for a further 25 minutes so that the centre and the apples are cooked through.
6) Remove the cake from the oven and test that it is cooked by inserting a skewer which should come out clean rather than sticky.
7) Cool the cake in the tin for an hour and then ease the cake out of the tin, still on the metal base and let it get cold. Place a large plate over the top of the cake and tip it upside down and then remove the paper.
8) Now place a plate over the base and tip the cake the right way up. Serve or store in an airtight container on the plate.

FRENCH VANILLA MACAROONS

Soft, sweet and slightly chewy these Ladurée-style macaroons are usually filled with ganache and come in lots of pretty colours. You can have fun changing the colour of your macaroons with a few drops of food colouring. You can experiment with flavours for the filling too but use tiny amounts to prevent curdling. Makes 12

75g/2³/4oz/³/4 cup ground almonds
115g/4oz/1 cup icing sugar
2 large egg whites
55g/2oz/¹/4 heaped cup caster sugar

Filling
55g/2oz dairy-free sunflower spread
85g/3oz/³/4 cup icing sugar, sifted
food colouring (optional)

•• You will need an oven size baking sheet or 2x smaller ones lined with non-stick baking paper or Teflon sheet and a 1cm/¹/2in piping nozzle with piping bag or a teaspoon.
•• Preheat oven to 200C/400F/Gas 6.

1) Put the ground almonds and icing sugar into a food processor. Blend to a fine powder and set aside.

2) Whisk the egg whites in a large clean bowl until they form firm peaks then add the sugar, 1 tablespoon at a time. Whisk well between each addition until the mixture is stiff.

3) Sift the almond mixture into the egg whites and fold in gently. If you are using food colouring add it now, a drop at a time until you achieve the desired colour. Fill the piping bag with the mixture and squeeze out 24 x 50 pence-sized macaroons. Space them evenly on the baking sheet/s.

4) Put the macaroons in the oven and immediately reduce the temperature to 150C/300F/Gas 2 and bake for 20 minutes. Half way through cooking time swap the baking sheets around to ensure even cooking.

5) Meanwhile, make the filling: In a small bowl gently and briefly mix the sunflower spread with the icing sugar until smooth. If you over mix, it risks curdling. Keep the mixture cool until needed.

6) Remove the macaroons from the oven and leave to cool, do not touch the macaroons until cold. Sandwich them together with the filling and serve or keep cool until needed.

ORANGE AND CHOCOLATE FINGERS

This recipe is adapted from one of my daughter's cookbooks and is easy and quick so don't be alarmed that you need a piping bag. If you don't have one you can make rounds with a teaspoon instead. Makes 24

225g/8oz dairy-free sunflower spread
55g/2oz/1/2 cup icing sugar
175g/6oz/11/2 cups Doves Farm gluten-
    free plain flour
55g/2oz/1/2 cup pure cornflour

Few drops pure vanilla extract
Grated zest 2 unwaxed oranges
100g/31/2oz Kinnerton Luxury Dark
    Chocolate

•• You will need a piping bag and nozzle.
•• Preheat the oven to 180C/350F/Gas 4.

1) Line a large baking sheet with baking parchment or Teflon sheet.
2) Cream together the sunflower spread and the icing sugar in a bowl.
3) Add the flour, cornflour, vanilla and orange zest and beat with a wooden spoon until light and fluffy.
4) Put the mixture into a piping bag fitted with a wide star nozzle. Pipe the mixture in short lines about 7cm/3in long. Bake in the centre of the oven for 15 minutes until pale golden.
5) Cool the biscuits on a wire rack. Break the chocolate into a small heatproof bowl and melt it over a small pan of simmering water.
6) When the biscuits are cold you can dip one end of each biscuit into the melted chocolate and lay it on the wire rack until the chocolate has set.

MARSHMALLOW SQUARES

I have spent some time recently researching cake decorations as I was amazed that so many had wheat in them. I went on a hunt and managed to find a small selection including mini marshmallows for decorating cupcakes. This recipe is for children and my daughter has fun making them especially if you use multicoloured marshmallows. Makes 24

200g/7oz packet of mini marshmallows
    (check they are gluten free)
100g/31/2oz dairy-free sunflower spread

1/2 teaspoon pure vanilla extract
175g/6oz gluten-free toasted puffed rice
    cereal

•• Grease 18cmx28cm/7x11in non-stick baking tin with a little extra sunflower spread or non-stick Teflon liner.

1) Put 175g/6oz of marshmallows into a medium sized pan with the sunflower spread and vanilla. Place it over low heat and cook until the ingredients have just melted, remove from the heat and set aside.
2) Roughly chop the remaining marshmallows.
3) Mix the rice cereal into the tepid melted mixture. Stir in the roughly chopped marshmallows. Spoon the mixture into the tray and press down with the back of a wooden spoon.
4) Allow to cool in the tray and cut into squares and store in an airtight container until needed.

CUPID CUPCAKES

These cupcakes can be decorated in any way you like but they make a lovely artistic gesture for St.Valentine's Day or Mother's Day. I have cheated and used ready made icing for speed but you can make your own. Makes 12

Weigh 3 medium eggs, note the weight
Weigh out the same amount each of
   Caster sugar
   Dairy-free sunflower spread
   And Orgran gluten-free self raising
   flour, sifted
1 teaspoon pure vanilla extract

Icing
225g/8oz/2 cups icing sugar sifted
30ml/2 tablespoons boiling water
Red food colouring
Dr. Oetker ready to roll coloured icing
   pack (125g/4$1/4$ oz each of red and
   yellow)
1 x packet Super Cook Select silver
   dragees
Sifted cornflour

- •• Preheat the oven to 190C/375F/Gas 4.
- •• You will need a small heart shaped cutter. Line a 12-hole muffin tin with cupcake cases.

1) Put the sugar and sunflower spread into the food processor and blend until light and fluffy. Add one egg and blend, add a teaspoon of the flour and blend and then add the remaining egg and vanilla.

2) Very briefly blend in the flour. Remove the blade for safety and scrape out 12 spoonfuls of the mixture into the prepared cases.

3) Bake them in the oven for 15 minutes until golden, firm and springy to the touch. Leave them to cool in the tin or on a wire rack. If the cakes are not flat then you need to slice off the tops so that they will be level for icing. You can use the tops for a trifle!

4) Put the sifted icing sugar in a bowl and add the water a little at a time, stirring until smooth. It should be thicker than double cream but not solid.

5) Add a few drops of red colour and mix until smooth and evenly coloured. Spread the red icing onto the cupcakes using a blunt knife dipped in hot water to smooth and shape.

6) Make sure you have clean hands and combine the ready to roll red icing with the yellow and squish and mould it into a lovely orange ball. When the colour is even then roll it out fairly thickly on a clean board dusted with a little sifted cornflour. Cut out 12 hearts and place each one in the centre of each cupcake using a drop of water to stick if the red icing has already set.

7) Place a silver dragee in the centre of each orange heart, this time you will definitely need a drop of water to stick them to the icing. Leave to set and package carefully as a gift or store in an airtight container.

VERY BERRY CAKE

This cake should keep for a week in an airtight container and so is very useful if you don't think that you will have enough time to make one during the various festive or holiday periods. It slices neatly for packed lunches too. Makes 1 large loaf

175g/6oz dairy-free sunflower spread

175g/6oz/1 cup caster sugar

4 medium eggs

150g/5oz/1¼ cups Orgran self raising flour

150g/5oz/1¼ cups Doves Farm self raising flour

170g/5½oz packet of Forest Feast dried berries and cherries or your own

mixture of dried cranberries, raisins, sour cherries and blueberries

130g/4½oz/1 cup ready-to-eat apricots, chopped

55g/2oz/¾ cup ground almonds

Grated zest and juice of 1 large unwaxed lemon

A little icing sugar for dusting

•• Preheat the oven to 170C/325F/Gas 3.
•• You will need a 1kg/2lb 2oz loaf tin, greased and floured or lined with non-stick baking paper.

1) Cream the sunflower spread and sugar in a food processor until light and fluffy. Gradually beat in the eggs and if it curdles then add a tablespoon of flour.
2) Scrape the mixture into a big bowl and fold in all the flour with all the dried fruit, ground almonds, lemon zest and juice.
3) Spoon into the prepared tin and lightly smooth the top. Bake in the oven for about 1½ hours until golden and firm to the touch.
4) Cool the cake in the tin until cold, if you turn it out warm then it might crumble when sliced. Turn the cake out onto a serving plate, dust the top with sifted icing sugar and serve.

PUDDINGS

This is my favourite section in any book as we love puddings and always have them at weekends and for parties. Somehow a pudding at the end of a meal gives your guests the impression that you are a good and generous cook! So well worth the extra time and effort. There are so many types of pudding that I decided to provide a cross section of all kinds of sweet treats, some hot and some cold to suit the seasons. I like to use local fruit for lots of my puddings so there are plenty of recipes for apples and the sort of fruit that you can easily buy at farmers' markets.

The best tip that I can give for choosing puddings is not to make them too heavy if you have already given your guests a hearty stew or roast. Try to vary the colours throughout the menu and don't have a pale starter and main course followed by a pale pudding or it will seem rather boring. Be wary of making a pudding that totally overwhelms the senses after a big luscious main course and to the other extreme you don't want to produce a very light starter and main course followed by a super light pudding or your guests will leave hungry!

Starting with the sponge puddings, I have chosen some rib sticking delights, the pear sponge is steamed in the traditional way, both the peach and the chocolate ones are baked in the oven and lastly the sticky toffee is baked and then covered in goo! Once you have made a steamed sponge and seen how simple it is then you can easily make steamed syrup, ginger, Christmas or other fruit puddings.

It was very tempting to include lots of chocolate recipes so much discipline was needed to have only four! I always think that if you can perfect two chocolate recipes for your repertoire then everyone will be happy. There is low-faff chocolate mousse and tart or high-faff profiteroles and hot puddings depending on your cooking skills. For the total beginner you cannot go wrong with dairy-free ice cream and chocolate sauce.

The best chocolate puddings are the result of using the best quality chocolate which is always clearly stated on the packaging by using percentages of cocoa solids. This sort of continental-style chocolate is usually more expensive with less sugar or none at all and less dairy or vegetable fat or none at all so that is does actually taste of chocolate. I have used Kinnerton Luxury Dark Chocolate because it is guaranteed to be nut, gluten and dairy-free which is a tall order and it does work extremely well in the recipes. But go and investigate and taste all sorts of chocolate and some flavoured ones too and find the one you like best. The lower the percentage of cocoa solids the less like good chocolate it will taste.

When cooking with chocolate you do have to be careful about overheating it. It should be melted in a heatproof bowl that will sit comfortably on top of a small or medium sized saucepan. The base of the bowl should be suspended a fair way from the base of the pan. Put about 2.5cm/1in of water in the pan and place the bowl over it. The water must not touch the bowl. Place over medium heat and then break up your chocolate into squares and put in the bowl. You can add any liquids that the recipe suggests. Once the water is simmering you can turn the heat off and let the bowl stand there until all the chocolate is melted. Stir from time to time. If the chocolate gets too hot, quickly sit the bowl in very cold water to cool down and avoid disaster. Stir out all the lumps and add a knob of butter/dairy-free spread if called for or follow the recipe. If the chocolate over-heats it seizes up like concrete and it is a lost cause to try and get it back to a smooth and runny state. Never mix anything cold into your melted chocolate as this will also make it seize up. Make sure the ingredients you add are room temperature and that the chocolate is lukewarm. Never add water or liquids at this stage or the same will happen.

I have used crumble mixture in two recipes as it is so easy to make that children can help too. The recipes use the crumble differently as the plum crumble has the crumble scattered on top to bake, but the apple crumble sundaes have the crumble in the middle. Nuts, seeds and porridge oats, if you are not intolerant to any of these ingredients, are ideal for making the crumble more interesting and ringing in the changes.

I hope that you will try out all the puddings and choose them to fit with the seasons and local ingredients for maximum satisfaction and pleasure.

ELDERFLOWER AND LEMON DRIZZLE CAKE

I was taking my wonderful Irish terrier for a walk down the lanes and saw so many beautiful elderflower blooms that yet again I could not resist making some cordial. As no one in my household will actually drink it, I decided to make a delicious pudding instead. Serves 8

175g/6oz dairy-free sunflower spread
175g/6oz/scant cup caster sugar
3 large eggs, beaten
200g/7oz/scant 1 3/4 cups Orgran self raising flour
4 tablespoons organic elderflower cordial
Juice and zest of 1/2 unwaxed lemon (unless you make your own cordial which will probably have plenty of lemon in it, then double the cordial instead)

Gooseberry Compote
500g/1lb 2oz fresh gooseberries, top and tailed
40g/1 1/2oz/1/4 cup caster sugar
To serve: Icing sugar, sifted
Swedish Glace dairy-free vanilla ice cream and gooseberry compote

•• Preheat the oven to 190C/375F/Gas 5.
•• 20cm/8in square cake tin, lined with a circle of baking parchment.

1) Cream the sunflower spread with the sugar in a mixing bowl until light and fluffy using a wooden spoon.
2) Beat in a spoonful of the egg at a time until about half is incorporated, this will prevent the mixture from curdling.
3) Mix one tablespoon of the flour into the mixture and then continue with the beaten egg.
4) Fold in the remaining flour. If the batter is not of dropping consistency then add in a tablespoon of hot water.
5) Carefully scrape the mixture into the tin and shake slightly to smooth and even the top. Never press the top with the back of the spoon or it will flatten the sponge.
6) Bake for about 35 minutes or until the cake is golden and the top is firm and springs back when touched with fingertips. Cool for 10 minutes in the tin and then turn out onto a serving dish.
7) Mix the 4 tablespoons of elderflower cordial with the lemon juice and zest. Alternatively just use 8 tablespoons of home-made elderflower cordial. Make lots of little holes with a skewer all over the warm sponge and then drizzle with the elderflower cordial.
8) Leave until cold, then dust with sifted icing sugar and decorate with flowers. Or cut into squares and serve each one with a scoop of ice cream and a spoonful of gooseberry compote.

•• To make gooseberry compote: Place the gooseberries in a pan; cook them with the sugar and over very low heat until soft and mushy. If too hot the sugar will caramelize and spoil the flavour.

MELTING CHOCOLATE PUDDINGS

This is the most popular pudding that I make for dinner parties. Guests are still impressed with this miracle of light sponge and oozing chocolate. Serves 6

185g/6¹/₂oz Kinnerton Luxury Dark
   Chocolate, roughly chopped
185g/6¹/₂oz dairy-free sunflower spread,
   plus extra for greasing
3 large eggs plus 3 extra egg yolks

6 tablespoons unrefined golden caster sugar
3 teaspoons Doves Farm gluten-free plain
   flour
Sieved cocoa powder (check label for dairy
   free) for dusting

- 6 large individual tin pudding moulds, fluted moulds or large ramekins lined with a circle of baking parchment.
- Preheat the oven to 220C/425F/Gas 7.

1) Melt the chocolate and sunflower spread in a heatproof bowl over a pan of simmering water, stirring occasionally until smooth and glossy.
2) In a separate bowl, whisk the eggs, yolks and sugar until thickened.
3) Whisk in the melted chocolate mixture and sieve and fold in the flour. Divide the mixture between the prepared moulds.
4) Bake the puddings for 12 minutes until the outside is set but the inside is still runny.
5) Carefully turn each pudding out onto a warm plate and serve with a dusting of cocoa powder.

- This is delicious served with a scoop of dairy-free vanilla ice cream

PANNA COTTA WITH RASPBERRY PURÉE

When I produced this recipe at a big recipe tasting dinner party everyone was amazed that you could even make a panna cotta without dairy. My little daughter who has the most sensitive taste buds pronounced this as good as a dairy recipe so I was completely reassured and here it is. Serves 6

4¹/2 level teaspoons gelatine
500ml/18fl.oz/2 cups unsweetened dairy-
   free soya milk
1 vanilla pod, split
40g/1¹/2 oz/³/4 cup caster sugar
250ml/9fl.oz/1 cup dairy-free soya single
   cream

1 teaspoon pure vanilla extract
Splash of orange-style liqueur/ Disaronno
   (amaretto) or rum
400g/14oz frozen raspberries, defrosted
   (or fresh in season)
Icing sugar to taste
Optional: **Extra berries for decoration**

•• You will need six large ramekins.

1) Put the gelatine into a cup or jug and pour in 4¹/2 tablespoons of just boiled water. Stir from time to time until the liquid is dissolved and clear.

2) Pour the soya milk into a pan. Scrape all the seeds out of the vanilla pod with the end of a teaspoon and then place the seeds and the pod into the milk.

3) Bring the milk to the boil over medium heat and then remove from the heat. Stir in the sugar. Retrieve the vanilla pod and wash it in very hot water until it is clean. Keep it for making vanilla sugar or custard.

4) Now stir the gelatine into the milk. Stir in the cream, vanilla extract and the liqueur or rum. Strain the mixture through a fine sieve into a mixing bowl or jug and then pour the panna cotta mixture into each ramekin.

5) Cover with cling film and refrigerate for at least 4 hours. Although they will set quite quickly the panna cotta will taste much better cold.

6) Make the raspberry purée by putting the raspberries, some icing sugar and water for fresh ones or use the defrosted juices from frozen berries until you have your desired consistency and taste.

7) Pass the sauce through a sieve with the back of a wooden spoon and discard the pips. Adjust the sweetness of the sauce to your liking and transfer to a jug or bowl and chill until needed.

8) To turn out each panna cotta simply run a very sharp small knife around the edges and place the ramekin onto the centre of a pudding plate. Give a brief shake to help release the panna cotta onto the plate. Lift off the ramekin and decorate the panna cotta with drizzles of raspberry purée and a few berries and serve or refrigerate until needed.

BAKED PEACH PUDDING

This pudding makes a nice change from the more traditional recipe using apples but you can use nectarines or ripe plums. Serve with dairy-free vanilla ice cream or vanilla custard. Serves 6

6 ripe peaches, peeled, quartered and stones removed
4 heaped teaspoons demerara sugar
1 vanilla pod, scored lengthwise and seeds removed

125g/4^1/2oz dairy-free sunflower spread
125g/4^1/2oz/^{2}/3 cup caster sugar
2 large eggs
125g/4^1/2oz/scant 1^1/4 cup gluten-free self raising flour, sifted plus a little extra

•• Preheat the oven to 180C/350F/Gas 4.

1) First pop the peaches into a bowl of boiling water and make a short slash in the skin with a sharp knife. Leave for a few minutes until you can easily peel off the skin. Drain the water, peel off the skin and discard.
2) Put the peaches, demerara sugar, vanilla seeds and 4 tablespoons of water into a large saucepan. Simmer over medium heat for 5 minutes.
3) Grease an ovenproof baking dish with sunflower spread and lightly flour it. Transfer the peaches and their juices to the dish.
4) In a bowl beat the sunflower spread and caster sugar until light and fluffy. Beat in the eggs, add the flour and gently fold in.
5) Lightly spoon blobs of the mixture over the peaches. Bake in the oven for about 35 minutes or until the sponge is set and golden. Remove from the oven and serve warm.

BAKEWELL TART

This classic English recipe is usually used as a cake at afternoon tea or coffee time but when it is made with really good jam and served with a scoop of dairy-free ice cream it is a great pudding. Serves 6-8

Shortcrust pastry (recipe page 119)
Filling
255g/9oz dairy-free sunflower spread
255g/9oz/1+1/3 cup caster sugar
300g/10oz ground almonds

3 medium eggs, beaten
5 tablespoons of really good strawberry or
    raspberry jam
A handful of sliced/flaked blanched
    almonds

•• Preheat the oven to 180C/350F/Gas 4.
•• You will need 24cm/9¹/2in loose-bottomed deep tart tin.

1) Make the pastry, chill and line the tin according to the instructions. Chill for 1 hour.
2) Bake the pastry tart for about 20 minutes or until light gold in colour. Remove from the oven and reduce the oven heat to 170C/325F/Gas 3.
3) Make the frangipane filling: beat the sunflower spread in a large bowl with the sugar until light and creamy and then beat in the almonds. Beat in the eggs until smooth. Chill for 20 minutes.
4) Smear jam all over the pastry base, pour over the chilled frangipane mixture and sprinkle with the flaked almonds. Bake the tart for about 55 minutes or until the mixture is firm and golden but still soft in the middle.

•• Leave to cool for an hour before serving warm or serve cold.

PLUM CRUMBLE

Crumbles are brilliant family puddings which can be varied throughout the seasons and are inexpensive and easy to prepare even in large quantities. I have often used this recipe to make an apple crumble for 8. Serves 6

Crumble topping
100g/3¹/₂oz/scant cup brown rice flour
30g/1oz/¹/₃ cup Orgran self raising flour
55g/2oz/¹/₃ cup pure cornflour
85g/3oz dairy-free sunflower spread
85g/3oz/¹/₂ cup soft brown sugar
85g/3oz/³/₄ cup chopped nuts (walnuts, pecans, hazelnuts, Brazil nuts or almonds or any mixture)

Filling
1kg/2lb 2oz ripe plums, halved, stalks and stones removed
1 teaspoon ground cinnamon
2 teaspoons rice flour
2 teaspoons dairy-free sunflower spread

•• Preheat the oven to 180C/350F/Gas 4.

1) Place the rice flour and the self raising flour with the cornflour in a large mixing bowl, add the sunflower spread and rub into the flour lightly with your fingertips.
2) When the mixture looks crumbly and the fat has been evenly distributed, add the sugar and nuts and combine.
3) Lightly poach the plums with the cinnamon in a covered dish inside the oven at the given temperature until soft or in a saucepan over gentle heat.
4) Mash the rice flour with the sunflower spread in a small cup and then gently stir into the hot mixture.
5) Pour the plum mixture into a deep oven-to-table baking dish. I suggest 24cm/9¹/₂in square as a good size. Spoon the crumble mixture evenly over the top and bake for 35 minutes or until golden with some oozing juices.
6) Serve warm with custard (see page 22) or a dairy-free vanilla ice cream.

LEMON TART

The sweet flan pastry recipe on page 120 is a perfect pastry for this recipe. The pastry needs to be thin, crisp, and buttery with an almost sweet shortbread texture. This is why we don't use a traditional shortcrust pastry in this tart or the chocolate tart. The size of lemons vary so much that I have specified the quantity of juice to ensure that the balance of sharpness and sweetness is perfect. Serves 8-10

Sweet pastry, see recipe page 120
Lemon filling
6 large eggs
250g/9oz/1+1/3 cup golden caster sugar
3-5 unwaxed lemons (total 175ml/6fl.oz/
   3/4 cup strained juice) and use the zest
   of 3 of the lemons

150ml/1/4 pint/1/2 cup dairy-free soya
   single cream
Gluten-free flour for dusting
Icing sugar for sifting

•• You will need a 26cm/10in fluted metal loose-bottomed tart tin.
•• Preheat the oven to 180C/350F/Gas 4.

1) Make the pastry first. Carefully remove the dough. Wrap in cling film and chill for 20-30 minutes.
2) Meanwhile make your filling. In a large bowl, using a wooden spoon beat the eggs with the sugar. Then beat in the lemon zest and juice.
3) Flour a clean board or area of your kitchen worktop. Place the dough in the centre of the floured area and flour your rolling pin.
4) Roll out the dough into a large enough circle to line the tin. The pastry should loosely sit on the tin and then you can gently work the pastry into the base and the edges.
5) Press the pastry into the flutes so that it rises above the tin as this will help prevent too much shrinkage. Lightly roll the rolling pin over the top of the tin to neaten off the edges.
6) Prick the base lightly with a fork and chill for 10 minutes. Place a large circle of baking parchment into the tart and fill with baking beans. Put the pastry in the oven and bake blind for 10 minutes. The pastry should only be pale gold.
7) Remove the paper and beans and leave them to cool before putting them away. Return the pastry to the oven and cook for another 10 minutes so that the base is cooked.
8) Strain the filling into a large jug and stir in the cream. Take the pastry case out of the oven and carefully fill with the lemon mixture. Reduce the heat to 150C/300 F/Gas 3 and slide the tart back into the oven.
9) Bake the tart until the filling is just set with a tiny bit of wobble in the centre. Allow about 25 minutes and then remove from the oven and leave to cool.
10) Serve the Lemon Tart the same day, lightly dusted with icing sugar.

CHOCOLATE TART

This classic French tart is so decadent and rich but by using soya cream there are slightly fewer calories than using thick cream. I try and do what the French do which is to have an elegant, slim slice of tart and leave a forkful on my plate but I always succumb to temptation and finish the last bit! Serves 8-10

Sweet Tart Pastry recipe on page 120
Filling
2 large eggs
3 large egg yolks

45g/1^{1}/$_{2}$oz/scant ^{1}/$_{3}$ cup caster sugar
100g/3^{1}/$_{2}$oz dairy-free sunflower spread
250g/9oz Kinnerton Luxury Dark
    Chocolate, broken into pieces

•• You will need a 24cm/9in loose-bottomed fluted metal tart tin.
•• Preheat the oven to 180C/350F/Gas 4.

1) Make the pastry according to the instructions on page 120 keeping to the chilling and baking blind times exactly.
2) Make the filling by putting the eggs, yolks and sugar into a bowl and beat together with an electric whisk until really thick and fluffy.
3) Melt the sunflower spread with the chocolate in a small pan over very low heat. Stir until the mixture is smooth.
4) Pour the chocolate onto the egg mixture and briefly beat until well combined. Then pour the chocolate filling into the prepared pastry case.
5) Return the tart to the hot oven for 10 minutes or until the filling is nearly set, then remove and leave to cool.

•• It is delicious served with a scoop of dairy-free vanilla ice cream and a dusting of cocoa powder.

SUGAR-FREE CHOCOLATE MOUSSE

I made this recipe for a couple of diabetic friends and they still rave about it. The better quality the chocolate that you use the better the flavour and texture. We have several local chocolatiers who make and sell their hand-made chocolate in Ludlow and the local area and so I can vary the flavours, for example chilli or ginger chocolate, orange or exotic spiced chocolate. Serves 6-8

250ml/9fl.oz/1 cup soya dairy-free single cream

2x100g/3¹/₂oz bars of sugar-free dark Belgian or other good quality chocolate (make sure it is dairy and gluten-free), broken into squares

1 teaspoon high quality instant coffee granules (omit if using any of the suggested flavours of chocolate)

2 tablespoons good quality brandy or cognac

3 large egg yolks

30g/1oz dairy-free sunflower spread

2 large egg whites

•• You will need 6-8 small ramekins, espresso or small coffee cups.

1) Heat the soya cream in the pan until nearly boiling and remove from the heat.

2) Stir in the chocolate and coffee until melted. Stir in the brandy or cognac, followed by the egg yolks and quickly whisk in with a balloon whisk until smooth. If you hang about the egg yolks will cook and be lumpy. Stir in the sunflower spread.

3) Whisk the egg whites in a large bowl until stiff and then fold one tablespoon of the egg into the chocolate mixture using a metal spoon. Then fold the chocolate mixture into the bowl of egg whites, lightly smoothing the lumps out.

4) Pour the mixture into the ramekins or espresso/coffee cups and chill for about 3 hours until set.

STRAWBERRY CHEESECAKE

It is amazing to think that nowadays you can make a delicious light and creamy cheesecake which is not only gluten and dairy-free but nut-free too. It keeps in the refrigerator for a day which is a great help with parties. Serves 8-12

300g/11oz packet gluten, dairy and nut-free digestive-style biscuits (see stockists)

85g/3oz dairy-free sunflower spread, melted

85g/3oz/1/2 cup demerara sugar

Optional 1/2 teaspoon ground cinnamon or ginger

2x225g/8oz tubs Tofutti Creamy Smooth Original cream-style cheese

3 teaspoons pure vanilla extract

3 tablespoons soya dairy-free single cream

3 tablespoons caster sugar

11.7g sachet/1 tablespoon gelatine powder dissolved in 150ml/1/4 pint/1/2 cup plus 1 tablespoon boiling water, or the vegetarian equivalent

2 large egg whites, stiffly beaten

450g/1lb fresh strawberries, hulled and wiped clean

Strawberry jam to glaze

•• You will need 23cm/9in spring-form cake tin lined with baking parchment.
•• Preheat oven to 180C/350F/Gas 4.

1) Make the crust first. Break up the biscuits and process them in a food processor until they resemble coarse breadcrumbs. Transfer them to a large bowl.

2) In a small pan, heat the sunflower spread, sugar and spices, if using, until melted and then pour into the biscuit crumbs and mix thoroughly.

3) Spoon the crumb mixture into the lined tin and press down hard until it is flat and even. Bake in the oven for about 20 minutes; remove from the oven and leave to cool.

4) When the base is cold make the filling. Place the cheese, vanilla, soya cream and sugar in a large bowl and mix until creamy and smooth.

5) Stir in the dissolved gelatine and then fold in the beaten egg whites. Spoon the mixture over the base and smooth over. Chill until firmly set.

6) Dip a knife in boiling water and quickly go round the cheesecake so that you can open and lift off the tin ring without taking any of the cheesecake with you. Slide a palette knife under the base so that you can slide the cheesecake off the lining paper onto a serving plate.

7) Cover the whole of the top of the cheesecake with halved or sliced strawberries working from the edge inwards. Warm some jam in a small pan and then brush it lightly all over the strawberries. Chill until needed.

APPLE CRUMBLE SUNDAES

Layers of apple, crunchy crumble and ice cream are piled up in tall old fashioned sundae glasses for a cool retro feel. The butterscotch sauce keeps for ages so that you can use it in other recipes too, such as the pancake recipe on page 49. Makes 4

8 eating apples, peeled, cored and chopped
Juice 1/2 lemon
55g/2oz/ scant 1/3 cup caster sugar
Crumble mixture
100g/31/2oz/scant cup Doves Farm
   gluten-free plain flour

55g/2oz dairy-free sunflower spread
55g/2oz/scant 1/3 cup demerara sugar

Butterscotch Sauce recipe on page 47
8 Scoops Swedish Glace dairy-free vanilla
   ice cream

•• Preheat oven to 200C/400F/Gas 6.
•• Line a baking tray with baking parchment.

1) Prepare the apples first and then make the crumble. Place the flour and sunflower spread in a bowl and rub them together with your fingertips until the mixture resembles fine breadcrumbs and mix in the demerara sugar.
2) Pour the mixture into the prepared baking tray, cook for 8 minutes until golden and leave to cool.
3) Meanwhile, gently cook the apples in the lemon juice with 4 tablespoons of water and the sugar. Add more water if necessary to prevent the purée sticking to the pan and to give a thick but smooth consistency. Cook until soft stirring from time to time and then leave the mixture to cool.
4) Break up the cooled crumble topping with a fork and set aside.
5) Make the butterscotch sauce and leave to cool.
6) Layer each sundae glass with cooked apple, crumble, ice cream and finally the butterscotch sauce. Serve immediately with long spoons!

LIME AND APPLE JELLIES

This is my idea of healthy fast food. Our local apples are so sweet and full of flavour that no sugar is needed but do add some if you need too. I made these for my daughter's Halloween party. We turned them out of the moulds and piped black icing spiders on them and some delightful worms! Makes 6 small moulds

1x135g/4^{1}/$_{2}$oz pack Hartley's Lime
   flavour jelly
About 8 eating apples, peeled, cored
   and chopped (to make 570ml/1pint/
   2^{1}/$_{2}$ cups)

Juice ^{1}/$_{2}$ large lemon

1) Break up the jelly squares and place them in a bowl and pour over 300ml/^{1}/$_{2}$pint/scant 1^{1}/$_{4}$ cups boiling water. Stir until the jelly has dissolved. Set aside to cool.

2) Meanwhile, very gently cook the apples in the lemon juice until soft; you will probably need to add a little water from time to time to prevent the apple becoming too dry and sticky. Remove them from the heat and beat the apples into a purée with a wooden spoon or balloon whisk.

3) Spoon the apple purée into the cooling jelly liquid and mix until smooth. Add a bit more boiled water if you don't think that the mixture will fill 6 jelly moulds. Refrigerate the jellies until set. Serve straight from the fridge. You can also turn the jellies out on to plates and serve with a scoop of dairy-free vanilla ice cream.

•• Grown ups love this jelly too, serve with dairy-free vanilla ice cream, a sprig of mint and ripe strawberries drizzled with a little fresh lime juice and zest.

TRADITIONAL APPLE PIE

Apple pie is an old time favourite here and in America, it is delicious with dairy-free vanilla ice cream or vanilla custard. Serve it warm or cold but I think that the filling should be simple without too many flavours. You can use frozen/defrosted cooked apple slices from the freezer. Serves 4-6

Shortcrust pastry, double the quantity on
  page 119
Filling
1kg/2lb 2oz Bramley or fresh eating apples
1 small egg white

140g/5oz/3/4 cup golden caster sugar and
  a bit extra
1/2 teaspoon cinnamon powder
2 tablespoons Doves gluten-free plain flour
  and a little extra

- You will need 24cm/9¹/2in pie tin.
- Preheat the oven to 180C/350/Gas 4.

1) Make the pastry and following the chilling time instructions.
2) Quarter, peel and core the apples and then slice them to about 5mm/¹/4in thick. Set aside in a large bowl.
3) Lightly beat the egg white in a bowl with a fork.
4) Roll half the pastry on a floured board with a floured rolling pin into a large circle and lift it over the pie tin and line the tin. Leave a slight overhang.
5) Flour the board and rolling pin again and roll out the remaining pastry into a circle wide enough to fit over the top of the pie.
6) Toss the apples with the sugar, cinnamon and flour. Pile them high into the lined pie tin. Brush the pastry rim with cold water and lay the lid over the top of the pie. Press the edges together to seal.
7) Trim the edges with a sharp knife and make 5 tiny slashes in the pastry lid to let the steam escape. Brush the pie with the beaten egg white and sprinkle with a little sugar.
8) Bake for about 50-60 minutes until the pastry is golden and the apples are soft. Set aside for 15 minutes, sprinkle with extra sugar and serve.

STEAMED SYRUP AND PEAR SPONGE

Seriously sticky and quite time consuming to get the paper and string organized but worth it. Watch out when you top up the water level that you don't get hit by any spluttering water or the steam. You could change the flavour to orange or lemon by adding finely grated zest or finely chopped stem ginger and powdered ginger would be delicious. Serves 6

225g/8oz dairy-free sunflower spread plus extra for greasing
3 large conference pears, peeled, halved and cored
8 heaped tablespoons golden syrup
225g/8oz/1 cup caster sugar

2 large eggs and 1 large egg yolk
200g/7oz/1 3/4 cup Orgran gluten-free self raising flour
1/2 teaspoon each grated nutmeg and ground cinnamon

•• You will need a greased 1.5litre/2 1/2 pint pudding basin and a greased sheet of baking parchment and enough string to tie around the bowl and make a handle.

1) Heat 25g/1oz of sunflower spread in a frying pan and cook the pears over medium heat for 5 minutes on each side until golden. Add 2 tablespoons syrup and simmer for 5 minutes until the sauce begins to caramelize. Leave to cool.

2) In a large bowl, beat the remaining sunflower spread with the sugar using an electric hand whisk until it is pale and creamy. Add the eggs and yolk, whisking thoroughly and lastly mix in the flour and spices at a more gentle speed.

3) Pour 3 tablespoons of golden syrup into the basin, spreading a little up the sides if you can. Spoon about 1/4 of the pudding mixture onto the syrup and arrange the pears one by one all around the sides of the basin with the cut side facing outward and their tips facing upward.

4) Use a spatula to spoon the rest of the pudding mixture into the centre of the pears in the basin, ensuring that some of the mixture fills the gaps between the pears. You might need to encourage the pears to stay put as you do this, just use your fingertips.

5) Cover with a large round of the greased paper, making a neat pleat across the middle. This allows the pudding to expand during cooking. Double up a length of string. Tie it around the top of the basin, threading the cut ends through the loop. Tie a knot and then take the length of string over the top of the basin and tie securely on the other side to make a handle. This will prevent burnt fingers when extracting the pudding from the steaming pan.

6) Fill the pan with enough boiling water to reach about half way up the pudding basin. Cover tightly with a lid and simmer for 2 hours topping up the water level when needed. Let the pudding rest for 10 minutes before turning out so that it doesn't fall to pieces and serve with the remaining syrup drizzled over the top.

STICKY TOFFEE PUDDINGS

I love these little puddings because you can freeze them in an ovenproof dish with the sauce poured all over them. You can then defrost them and reheat covered in some oiled foil and in a hot oven for about 15-20 minutes. They are delicious with dairy-free vanilla ice cream or custard. Makes 7

225g/8oz whole dates or ready chopped
175ml/6fl.oz/scant 3/4 cup boiling water
1 teaspoon pure vanilla extract
175g/6oz/1+ 2/3 cup Orgran gluten-free
  self raising flour, plus 1 tablespoon extra
1 teaspoon bicarbonate of soda
85g/3oz dairy-free sunflower spread, plus
  extra for greasing
140g/5oz/3/4 cup demerara sugar
2 large eggs

2 tablespoons black treacle
125ml/4fl.oz/1/2 cup dairy-free
  unsweetened soya milk
Toffee sauce
175g/6oz/1+1/3 cup light muscovado sugar
55g/2oz dairy-free sunflower spread
225ml/ scant cup dairy-free soya single
  cream
2 tablespoons black treacle

•• Preheat the oven to 180C/350F/Gas 4.
•• You will need 7 mini pudding tins or large ramekins.

1) Stone and chop the dates, put them in a bowl and pour boiling water over them. Leave them for about 30 minutes until cool and well soaked and mash with a fork.
2) Stir in the vanilla extract. Grease and flour the tins or ramekins and set them in a large baking tray.
3) Put the flour and bicarbonate of soda in one bowl and the sunflower spread and sugar in another. Beat the spread and sugar together until light and creamy. Beat the eggs in a jug or bowl and then beat a little at a time into the sugar mixture.
4) Beat in the black treacle and then using a metal spoon lightly fold in 1/3 of the flour followed by half the soya milk. Repeat until the flour and milk are used up. Stir in the soaked dates and you will have a rather curdled soft batter.
5) Spoon the mixture into the prepared tins or ramekins and bake for about 20 minutes or until risen and firm.
6) Meanwhile, put the sugar and sunflower spread for the toffee sauce in a pan with half the soya cream. Bring to the boil over medium heat, stirring all the time until the sugar has completely dissolved. Stir in the black treacle and turn up the heat to let the mixture bubble and boil for 3 minutes until it has a rich toffee colour.
7) Stir occasionally to make sure that it doesn't burn, take the pan off the heat and stir in the remaining soya cream.
8) Remove the puddings from the oven and leave in their tins for about 10 minutes. Loosen them from the sides with a small knife before turning them out. Serve them on warm plates with the sauce drizzled over.

Useful Addresses and Stockists

Institute for Optimum Nutrition
Avalon House
72 Lower Mortlake Rd
Richmond
TW9 2JY
Telephone: 0870 979 1133

The Coeliac Society
3rd Floor, Apollo Centre
Desborough Road
High Wycombe
Buckinghamshire
HP11 2QW
Telephone: 01494 437278
Allergy Alerts
This is a free text and email alert service for
people with food allergies. It sends out alerts
when products are contaminated by nuts, dairy
or gluten. Privacy is guaranteed and most
people only receive a handful of alerts each
year but one might be a life saver! Register
free at w**ww.alert4allergy.org**

**I have spent years testing different brands
of products and I find that the following
brands consistently prove to be the best.**

Wellfoods Ltd
(Antoinette Savill signature series)
This is a nationwide delivery of freshly baked
gluten-free products. The large white loaf
freezes very well especially when pre-sliced
and wrapped in individual or double portions.
The pizza bases, bread rolls, burger buns and
other products also freeze well. The flour is
very white and light to use.
Telephone: 01226 381712
Website: **www.bake-it.com**

The Village Bakery
(organic breads and cakes)
These are my favourite rye breads and they
make a good selection of gluten and wheat-
free seasonal and other cakes, biscuits and
sponges.
Telephone: 01768 898437
Website: **www.village-bakery.com**

Provamel Alpro (UK) Ltd
(milks and yoghurts)
This is my favourite soya milk and cream –
I find that the taste, colour and consistency is
by far the best. The yoghurts are good too.
Telephone: 01536 720605
Website: **www.provamel.co.uk**

Tofutti UK Ltd (cheeses)
This seems to be the best range of dairy-free
cream-style cheese dips. The Sour Supreme
sour cream substitute is also very good for
cheesecakes and dips. I keep a supply of ice
creams in the freezer throughout the year.
Telephone: 020 8861 4443
Website: **www.tofutti.com**

The Redwood Wholefood Company
(cheeses)
My favourite is the Greek/feta-style which is
brilliant on pizzas, pasta, risotto, stuffed allergy-
free pitta breads and salads.
Telephone: 01536 400 557
Website: **www.redwoodfoods.co.uk**

Orgran Community Foods Ltd
(pasta, self raising flour and breadcrumbs)
They have the biggest variety of pasta shapes,
the most useful for children being the
macaroni which is bite size. I am a great fan of
the breadcrumb alternative for making fish
cakes, chicken nuggets and the flour for cakes.
Telephone: 01455 556 878
Website: **www.communityfoods.co.uk**

Doves Farm Foods (flour and cookies)
I use their buckwheat, rice, plain and self raising flours throughout the recipes. The delicious Lemon Zest Cookies are an ideal treat occasionally but also make the best biscuit bases for cheesecakes.
Telephone: 01488 684 880
Website: **www.dovesfarm.co.uk**

Kinnerton Confectionery
Great dairy, nut and gluten-free chocolate with all year round novelties and suitable decorations for gifts. The best chocolate that I have found for making chocolate tarts, sauces, mousses, cakes and cookies.
Telephone: 020 7284 9500
Website: **www.kinnerton.com**

Swedish Glace (ice creams)
Very good ice creams which are not only gluten free but also lactose, cholesterol and GM free. Both the smooth vanilla and rich chocolate are great in a pavlova, as a filling for profiteroles or with chocolate, butterscotch or fruit sauce. Wild blueberry or raspberry also works very well with the meringues.
Telephone : 01270 589311
Website: **www.fayrefield.com**

Parmesan replacer
Life Free From, dairy-free Parmazano is a grated mature hard cheese replacer and based on non-GM soya and vegetable oil. It is not only vegetarian and vegan but also safely nut, gluten and lactose free. A little goes a long way.
Telephone: 01322 337711
Website: **www.parmazano.com**

Meridian
Produces endless good products such as no added sugar fruit spreads, gluten-free spicy sauces, a good green and a red pesto and passata.
Telephone: 01962 761935
Website: **www.meridianfoods.co.uk**

Lovemore Free From Foods
Fabulous frozen puff pastry and sausage rolls. Delivered frozen and ready to use. Delicious mince pies, cheese straws and cake slices.
Telephone: 0800 0255678
Email: admin@welshhills.com
Website: **www.lovemore-freefromfoods.com**

Sally's Sizzling Sausage Co.
Fantastic gluten-free sausages that you can freeze and also use for the sausage rolls recipe if you remove the skin. You can replace the venison sausage recipe with the hot and spicy or the pork and apple variety.
Email: enquiries@sallyssizzlers.com
Website: **www.sallyssizzlers.com**

Drossa Limited
This has to be the most up-market collection of gluten-free foods I have ever come across. The products are sourced from around the world and only the best will do. Amazing gnocchi, caper berries, tzatziki herb mix, cannelloni, red pesto and my favourite almond macaroons in all sorts of seductive flavours.
Telephone: 020 7431 9382
Website: **www.drossa.co.uk**

Index